IN PRAISE OF BONE

New and Selected Poems
(1991–2021)

Anand Thakore

SPEAKING TIGER BOOKS LLP
4381/4, Ansari Road, Daryaganj
New Delhi 110002

First published by Speaking Tiger Books in paperback in 2023

Copyright © Anand Thakore 2023

ISBN: 978-93-5447-563-4
eISBN: 978-93-5447-562-7

10 9 8 7 6 5 4 3 2 1

All rights reserved.
No part of this publication may be reproduced, transmitted, or stored in a
retrieval system, in any form or by any means, electronic,
mechanical, photocopying, recording or otherwise,
without the prior permission of the publisher.

This book is sold subject to the condition that it shall not, by way of trade
or otherwise, be lent, resold, hired out, or otherwise circulated,
without the publisher's prior consent, in any form of binding
or cover other than that in which it is published.

Praise for Anand Thakore's Poetry

'The control of movement and tightness of language in these poems would be remarkable in any young poet anywhere…' – **Dom Moraes, *Mid-Day*, 1995**

'Here is a gifted poet, of the calibre of Dom Moraes, who paints landscapes and seascapes with their flora and fauna in memorable lines while strictly observing rules of metre and rhyme which most modern poets tend to ignore…' – **Khushwant Singh, *Hindustan Times*, 2005**

'"Twelve tongues now congregate at the tip of my tongue / to lift the weight of my artless shout," says Babur, in one of the five sections that make up Anand Thakore's richly imagined *Mughal Sequence*. In work that is multi-tongued in its own way and far from artless, the poet reconstructs episodes from the lives not only of emperors but of a prophetic begum, a marginalised dancing girl and a gloomy Kohinoor diamond. Contemporary poetry abounds in poems on historical subjects, but I haven't read anything quite as ambitious and evocative as *Babur, After the Victory at Khanua*…' – **Adil Jussawalla on *Mughal Sequence*, 2012**

'Anand Thakore's verse has many of the qualities that I value in poetry: a richness and clarity of image, an assured musicality, a sensuous fascination with the "surfaces of things" as well as the fevered need to probe those surfaces, however beguiling, and "forage for meaning". These poems embody and explore interesting tensions: an almost oracular mode that is capable of swerving abruptly into the mock-heroic or vividly anecdotal; a repeatedly articulated need for stasis as well as the need for change; an impulse to craft a self and a world that is sovereign and inviolable and yet welcome a "stark and craftless rapture"; the urge to remain "sealed", "inanimate", "unhurt", and yet open out to surprise, danger, denouement and the inevitable journey "downhill and seawards".

Eventually, the age-old question of whether truth and beauty must be mutually exclusive, which churns in its own particular way at the heart of Thakore's work, is best stilled by the luminosity of metaphor—such as the image of an elephant's single tusk above the river-line, "white as a quarter-moon in mid-July / before the coming of a cloud."' – **Arundhathi Subramaniam on *Elephant Bathing*, 2012**

'Anand Thakore's *Mughal Sequence* invites us into a captivating musical arrangement: a quintet of voices drawn from the history of the Mughal dynasty; voices retrieved from the calligraphy of memoir and testament, their stresses and phrases recast, their habitual patterns adroitly reanimated. These poems render the past as a historical present, within which we find our own place as avid eavesdroppers or unwitting confessors. They remind us that to read is to listen; to attend as much with the cochlea as with the eye. Anand Thakore's *Mughal Sequence* is a splendid, magical achievement.' – **Ranjit Hostkote, preface to *Mughal Sequence*, 2012**

'There is a meditative streak about much of Anand Thakore's poetry. Whether it his personal past or the last sad days of a widower grandfather floating on "the oarless raft of his grief", or Karna ruminating on giving up his armour, the contemplative mode is ever present; and he is in the habit of "wading through the deepening swamp of the self". This also necessarily brings in more strands than one, so that a poem turns complex and becomes a "knotted cord". A poem on a wind chime ("this swirling welter of splintered thoughts") will end up by talking of space. A glacier moving downriver will make you think of destiny. The imagery is startling and sharp, as it should be in good poetry. This poetry is beyond the ephemeral. I am privileged to have read it.' – **Keki N. Daruwalla on *Elephant Bathing*, 2012**

'*Elephant Bathing* shows remarkable breadth, not only in its subject matter—which ranges from the domestic to the spiritual—but also in its style and use of form...Thakore's craftsmanship is accompanied by the rich musical quality of his writing. Each sentence is carefully balanced, and his use of alliteration and internal rhymes makes his work a particular pleasure to read aloud.' – **Emma Bird, on *Elephant Bathing*, *Wasafiri*, 2013**

'There are personal poems, poems that are narrative in intent, holding on to fugitive memories with the adult grip of words. There are explorations of form—the ghazal, the sonnet, the villanelle—but even when there is no apparent frame to hold the poem, Thakore never lets himself play tennis without some kind of net...*Elephant Bathing* and its sibling *Mughal Sequence* are offerings to savour and return to over many rewarding readings.' – **Sridala Swami, *Biblio*, 2013**

'"Time", critic Harold Bloom once wrote, "which decays and then destroys us, is even more merciless in obliterating weak poems, however virtuous they might be." Ultimately that impossible standard, seen from the vantage point of an imaginary future, must be brought to bear on ascertaining the worth of something like a "Selected Poems"—and very happily, Anand Thakore's poems, written over the course of twenty years, prove themselves to be expertly crafted, deeply felt, and profoundly musical verbal artefacts daring and durable enough to stand that ultimate test. There is something classical about his verse, his sonnets and villanelles, his rhyming quatrains and dramatic monologues, and yet they are never stiff; instead, they marry Tennyson's gift of cadence, Browning's mastery of voice, Donne's metaphysics, Kabir's iconoclasm and Keats' plunging into negative capability, all while retaining a wicked wit and signature style. Here's a poem that apostrophises a fondue pot, the melted cheese "thickening into a crust like some incurable grief,"—and one that eviscerates an aspiring surrealist so perfectly, it could be stand-up comedy. Here also is *Mughal Sequence*, one of the finest long poems composed in our times. Anand Thakore is that master wordsmith too little known outside of India and not even there as much as he deserves. His *Selected Poems* is a triumph.' – **Ravi Shankar on *Selected Poems 1992–2012*, 2016**

'Anand Thakore's verse exemplifies the art of masterly literary conceit, as voices from the world of the dead reach out and speak to us: a Tibetan monk who has committed suicide, a terrorist expressing his last wish before facing execution, a musician on his deathbed recounting some of the most important moments in his life. Thakore writes with amplitude—a near-baroque use of language. He gives each voice time to explore its needs, resulting in long poems that are replete with material. Nowhere does the poet slacken his tempo and there is admirable control over meter. The tension in thought and music carries us effortlessly from page to page. This book is a welcome and wonderful addition to Thakore's growing body of work.' – **Gieve Patel on *Seven Deaths and Four Scrolls*, 2017**

*For the poets that kept me moving—Gieve, Adil, Arundhathi,
Keki and Dom; and the friends that saw me through—
Mohsin, Azaan, Sumeir and Ritu*

Contents

Introduction by Dr Ravi Shankar	xi
Author's Note	xxiii

NEW POEMS (2015–2021)

Obverse	3
Dawn at Lake Pangong	4
Joseph and Potiphar's Wife	5
Waterhole	7
Threesome	9
On Reading Richard II a Second Time	10
That's How It Feels	11
Sea Link	12
Nocturne at Afghan Church	13
Brazil	14
Two Miniatures	15
I. DIWALI ON THE PALACE ROOF	15
II. SUDAMA TAKES KRISHNA'S LEAVE	16
Horse Trainer	17
Man and Woman Gazing at the Moon	18
Standing Stone Saraswati, Twelfth Century, Deccan	19
Constantinople, 1453	20
I. ANGELUS OF A BYZANTINE COURTESAN	20
II. CONSTANTINE XI SEES A RED MOON RISE	21
Nuptials at Somaiya House	23
I. EPITHALAMION	23
II. NO PLACE FOR WOMEN	24
III. SOMAIYA HOUSE	26

Thamyris	28
Basic Winemaking for Beginners	29
Ringtone	31
Evidence	32
Hymns of a Broken Man	33
I. WATERSNAKE	33
II. MATINS	33
III. VIEW FROM A SHIVA SHRINE	34
Two Poems Borrowed from the Saints	36
I. THE NAME	36
II. THE FLUTE	37
Variation for Buddha Purnima	38
Lines to my Secret Mentor with a Verse by Emerson	39

FROM SEVEN DEATHS AND FOUR SCROLLS (2017)

'Puppet's Life Ends on String'	43
'Buddhist Monk Hangs Self'	45
SCROLL ONE	45
SCROLL TWO	48
SCROLL THREE	51
SCROLL FOUR	52
Death at the Opera Comique	54
Kamadeva Muses upon the Death of the Body	57
Holika	60

MUGHAL SEQUENCE (2012)

Mughal Sequence	65
I. HUMAYUN ATONES	65
II. GULBADAN BEGUM IN SURAT, EN ROUTE TO MECCA	70
III. DANCING GIRL	74
IV. BABUR, AFTER THE VICTORY AT KHANUA	77
V. THE KOH-I-NOOR	95

FROM ELEPHANT BATHING (2012)

Bitter Gourd	99
Nineteen Forty-two	100
Tidal Wave	102
Elephant Bathing	104
Dead, at Your Mother's Funeral	106
My Father's Old Man	107
Tusker Kills Mahout at Religious Festival	109
Ghazal	112
Negotiating Negativity on the Western Ghats	113
Glacier	114
Vacillations of a Recondite Nudist	116
Living Room	117
Steam Bath	118
Duet on the Death of a Cat	119
The Buddha Above the Window	120
Housewarming	122
Sequence Addressed to Hanging Objects	123
I. PUNCHING BAG	123
II. DREAM CATCHER	124
III. WIND CHIME	125
Apostrophe to a Fondue Pot	128
The Schoolboy on the Pont Alexandre III	135
Ostrich Egg	136
Hangman's Knot	138
The Sun Made Flesh	141
I. KUNTI REMINISCES	141
II. KARNA, ON GIVING UP HIS ARMOUR	143
Lament of an Onanist Bemused by the Void	146
Ablutions	147

FROM WAKING IN DECEMBER (2001)

Ithaca	151
To the Face of an Infant Seen through a Fish Tank	153
Creepers on a Steel Door	155
Departure	156
Toy Store Window	157
Nocturne	158
In Praise of Bone	159
To an Aging Sarod Player	160
Chandri Villa	161
Harbour Crossing	162
In Praise of Laterality	163
Monologue of a Piece of Coal	164
Kaleidoscope	165
Villanelle	167
The Thing Itself	168
Words to an Aspiring Surrealist	169
What I Can Get Away With	170
Study	172
Aubade	173
Water Cabbages	174
Lines to an Ex-Lover's Pet Tortoise	175
A Leave-Taking	178
Acknowledgements	180

Introduction

British neoclassical eighteenth-century poet Alexander Pope, one of the masters of the heroic couplet, begins the second epistle in 'Essay on Man':

Know then thyself, presume not God to scan,
The proper study of mankind is Man.
Placed on this isthmus of a middle state,
A being darkly wise and rudely great:
With too much knowledge for the Sceptic side,
With too much weakness for the Stoic's pride,
He hangs between, in doubt to act or rest.

Pope's words are appropriate when considering Indian poet Anand Thakore's considerable poetic achievement, because over the course of *In Praise of Bone*, he shows himself to be both darkly wise and rudely great—those oxymorons much more compatible than might initially appear—and he inherits the mantle of those great formalists among English-language poets for whom prosody is a serious business, an intricately built scaffolding upon which to fix thought against the flux and ravages of time. However, lest we imagine that this interest in formalism is bloodless and didactic and gimmicky, meted out with the dispassionate eye of a pharmacist titrating acids into vials, we find within *In Praise of Bone* poems that give voice to historical presences like Tulsidas, the sixteenth-century Bhakti poet of Rama, who describes himself as 'scrawny and dry as a leaf of cannabis', and we learn what it is like 'to get fucked awake by the dead'. No, this is no fusty, antiquated mind at work but a poet keenly aware of the vicissitudes of contemporary life, loss, family, eros, art and grief; universal themes, but what makes Thakore a particularly special poet is that while the tapestry he weaves upon is vast and numinous, historical in sweep, his evocations are granular with specificity and symbolism.

Take the opening of the eponymous poem of the collection, 'In Praise of Bone':

Somewhere at the back of the brain,
Is a place I will never go to again;
An old stone guardhouse long deserted,
And over the slow green spaces of a lily-pond skirted
By rock, quick breeze and a low murmur of reeds.
The rocks are large and flat. I look up from the weeds
Wedged between their edges; his eyes are too full of love.
…
Marrow will outlive its bone—
We are plant, animal, stone,
And everything we believe ourselves to be.
When the rain stops he only feels my skin
To know my bones are still the same shape;
The same hard forms we will never escape,
We know in the end only they can win:

The poem begins by complicating the much-derided rhyming couplet with the poetics of suggestion—what is that place at the back of the brain, where the edge of cranial tissue meets the cold, hard dome of skull, where consciousness is certain of its own mortality? Instead of verging into abstraction, the answer resides in the fluent lyric grace of the descriptions of the 'old stone guardhouse' and the 'slow green spaces of a lily-pond skirted / by rock'. The enjambment is pitch perfect, one line skirting another so that the rhyme is not forced but necessary; and in the slow green space we hear an echo of Andrew Marvell's 'The Garden':

The mind, that ocean where each kind
Does straight its own resemblance find,
Yet it creates, transcending these,

Far other worlds, and other seas;
Annihilating all that's made
To a green thought in a green shade.

There's also a variance of sentence structure, so that we move from a brocaded compound sentence to a short, declarative one ('The rocks are large and flat.'), and then the 'weeds / wedged between their edges', uses alliteration and internal rhyme again to wedge a perfect enjambment, the breaking of the line mirroring what is being described.

Whereas in Marvell's lines the mind is briny depth and metaphysically broken into the Cartesian duality of body and soul, in Thakore's lines, the mind is pure matter—'plant, animal and stone'—which is precisely *why* it matters; because the working of the will means that we can take on the mantle of any identity on earth; however, the skeletal certainty of our bodies' expiration, so similar, it turns out, to every other body in decomposition, even as we extravagantly emphasize our differences in life, is all that will remain in the end. Those are the 'hard forms we will never escape', which is precisely why the speaker does not want to return to the back of the brain.

Yet, this is not a macabre poem, because of the sensuality of the rain, the eroticism of two bodies growing 'as tangled as a banyan tree', the acceptance of the immutable facts of our life, and because Thakore, in essence, has invented a brand-new poetic model which resists the calcification of hard forms; for this memorable twenty-line poem is indeed a new species of couplet interbred with Petrarchan sonnet. The first ten lines are rhyming couplets, then there's a volta when the rain begins; the poem itself shifts into an entirely different rhyme scheme—AABB transmigrating to ABBA—and in that slight variance, we have our answer to the use of poetic form: patterned language fixes flux in place against the ravages of time.

Thakore's poems are permeated with this sense of aging and the addresses—to an aging sarod player, to a childhood home named for a man who died of the plague in 1919, to a father and grandfather, to a punching bag and a wind chime—share an elegant perspicuity, a keen attention to loss and a razor-edged wit. We see these qualities from his earliest work, from which the title poem 'In Praise of Bone' was taken, to his newest poems; and if his gaze has remained unflinching over the decades, his observation has evolved to include the technology of the world we live in now. While this manuscript alludes and counts as influence such figures as Ralph Waldo Emerson, Tulsidas, Shakespeare, Wallace Stevens, Surdas and Homer, he often uses bits of quotidian journalism as the impetus for his poems—an epigraph taken from a photo caption in *The Times of India* about an elephant run riot in Kerala or an article from *The New Indian Express* about a monk committing suicide in Chennai—proving that creativity can reside in the quotidian.

Thakore's newer work is more personal and intimate, addressed to former lovers and lost friends and family, and his sense of lineation has loosened over the years, so that we have the wonderfully jagged and moving lines of a poem like 'Waterhole'. That poem is in tercets, but less tightly buttoned than Thakore's earlier work, and for good reason, because the specter is of a dying father, lying in an ICU, 'his speech now taken from him / By bandages, tubes and pipes. / What wants to leap is like the sound and stroke / Of a bright steel plectrum against a taut tuned string'. Thakore's enjambments are again well-honed, particularly 'the sound and stroke', which conveys multiple connotations, the disease that robs the brain of its blood flow as well as the musician's careful strumming of his instrument. But this is no wanton metaphor, an image in place simply for its sensibility and sonic quality, for the speaker manages to connect this to his father's childhood and his slow reversion into the zoomorphic and onomatopoeic 'crane-squawk and deer-bark', where his only longing as his breath slows is for water. Powerful, poignant, heartbreaking stuff, but never glossed over with a facile sentimentality.

Thakore's newer poems include several ekphrastic poems, such as 'Two Miniatures,' which take on eighteenth-century Kishangarh and Chamba Valley miniature paintings, done in a tradition which traces back to at least the ninth century CE. Indian miniature paintings are minuscule in scale (often just a few inches in size) yet, highly detailed and individualistic; Kishangarh painting is an eighteenth-century Rajasthani-style of Indian art that is distinguished by intricate human forms, spiritual intensity and panoramic landscapes, and in Thakore's hands, we see the painter's attempt to freeze infinitesimal sparks in paint, just the way the poet does in words. 'Fire,' the poem asserts, 'is just another game night likes to play.'

However, showing his innate cosmopolitanism, Thakore doesn't stop at Indian paintings, but also writes ekphrastic verse about a Mongolian watercolour of a horse trainer that preserves 'the sudden, silent thud of brush and ink / Hoofprints on dunes, hoofbeats on paper', the synesthesia capturing the kinesis of an image we can almost see *and* hear in the poem; he writes about nineteenth-century German Romantic landscape painter Caspar David Friedrich whose allegorical work shows contemplative figures silhouetted against the night sky, 'their faces, because never painted, forever invisible'; and in my favourite, he writes about 'Standing Stone Saraswati, Twelfth Century, Deccan,' which is a kind of rejoinder to Rainer Maria Rilke's 'Archaic Torso of Apollo,' whose legendary head with eyes like ripening fruit we can never know. Many of the Buddhist, Hindu and Jain monuments in the Deccan peninsula were defaced by Islamic armies who found the anthropomorphic figures offensive. This poem begins:

Victim of a faith that will never understand her,
    Defaced, mastectomised, her many arms mutilated,
Then left to lie at the bottom of a pond for centuries,

She is now object who once was divine—
    Her face flattened featureless,
Her stone lute lost, her right leg a cleft,

Bare ridges of quarried rock where garlanded breasts
> Once brazenly hung.

No sign remains here now, upon the cratered waist and torso,

Or amidst these tides of bruised rock, round chunks of shoulder,
> Shards of a bracelet, shreds of an elaborate girdle,

To remind us that this indeed is she: white-robed matriarch,

Virgin, patroness and progenitor of all speech and song.

Unlike Rilke's Apollo, this desecration does not burst like a star from all the borders of itself; instead, it is a potent, persistent reminder of misogyny, for only the peacock at her feet survives but the goddess herself has been destroyed. The Hindu goddess Saraswati is the patron of the arts and language and knowledge, her name deriving from the Sanskrit word for 'that which is fluid'. She is the perfect muse for a poet and if her sculptural form had been preserved then we might have glimpsed that she has four hands, two of which play the veena while the other two hold scripture and a lotus, embodiments of an aesthetic, spiritually attuned life. Of course, the marauders didn't see it that way and chose to mutilate this sculpture for her embodiment of the female form, preserving only this plumed bird, which was not a 'serious threat to the invader's abstract monolithic order, / Unworthy of his victorious, descending axe'.

    With such fluent ease, Thakore can fold in centuries worth of history into his verse; we enter Constantinople in 1453 and sit under the lamplit arch of Afghan Church, built in Mumbai in 1858 to honour the British soldiers who died in the prolonged failed military campaigns against Afghanistan: 'syllables of stone that praise a resplendent defeat'. Yet, lest we imagine that these digressions into the past are all rendered in one tone, one mode of looking, his books *Seven Deaths and Four Scrolls* and the monumental *Mughal Sequence*, demonstrate his range, for like so many great artists, from Thelonious Monk and Gerhardt Richter, Thakore never settles for a singular reflexive gaze, but constantly evolves his vision and intention. These collections provide us a vista into the past via the vehicle of the dramatic monologue.

In the excerpts from these collections, the poet takes on many voices, such as that of a twenty-four-year-old Buddhist monk who committed suicide in Chennai, expanding his imagined anguish into four scrolls. Thakore's imagistic brilliance is on full display here, and we are 'caught in this blizzard of images that spin like prayer-wheels'; images that include 'smell of sweat and incense', 'hoofprints of ponies on unscalable glaciers', 'the gaping, cadaverous lips of mountain-tunnels', and 'unyielding car-horns and juddering motors'. Tunefully, we move from the olfactory to the kinesthetic to the gustatory to the auditory, each image carrying Ezra Pound's dictum that it carry 'an intellectual and emotional complex in an instant of time'. Moreover, this pulsating and visceral sensuality is at odds with a Buddhist monk's renunciation of sensory pleasure. The poem continues:

Here, amidst all I must let go of to move ahead,
With the drone of young rivers and the smell of yak-fur,
The first faces recur, like audible fragments

Of a chant one assumes unbroken.
I sense in their gaze the hurt I caused them,
And the unaltered presence of parental will;

…

There remains, on my part, the searing presence
Of so much I could hold myself accountable for—but no,
I did not choose a life that denies the flesh,

The cheerless fellowship of the sash and shaven head,
The life of the rosary, robe and silent room,
Any more than I chose the hand I died by.

The philosophical complication this poem proposes is richly paradoxical (for how could someone who committed suicide say that it was not their very own choice?)—yet, it is always firmly anchored in memories of a childhood in Ladakh and in the urban life of Chennai, the world of young rivers and yak milk contrasted with 'clouds of exhaust and cement dust' and 'corrugated cement streaked with blue plastic'. And in that juxtaposition, this localized voice suddenly becomes universal—for who among us does not remember a simpler time, or a choice about our own lives we were not given, or the way cultural forces conspire to have us all conform, whether our role is to be an accountant or a monk?

There's another poem in the voice of Kamadeva, the Hindu god of desire, and Holika, an *asura*, or demoness and embodiment of evil whose death is celebrated ritualistically in a bonfire before Holi, the ancient Hindu festival of colours. Shifting persona and diction, putting on different masks, Thakore reveals parts of himself that could not otherwise have been seen. The *Mughal Sequence* is further evidence of his mastery of that most arduous of forms: the long poem. As the critic Stephanie Burt writes, 'they [long poems] use length as an aesthetic device: their continuity, their ongoingness, shows how the people, things, feelings they depict remain intertwined, open-ended, hard to resolve. Because they can take the time to show you how to read them, they depend less than brief lyric poems do on conventions you're likely to understand coming in. They have room to digress: they have space to double back, and even to string you along.'

The *Mughal Sequence* does just that, layering voice upon voice so that we have a shimmering tapestry that while preserving and giving voice to Indian history also shares an intimate personal narrative taken from each individual character—we hear from Humayun, the second emperor of the Mughal Empire; we hear from his half-sister, Gulbadan Begum, daughter of Emperor Babur, the founder of the Mughal Empire, and whose written account of her half-brother's life informs much of what we know about him today; we hear from a dancing girl who was given as a royal gift to a Begum and who 'scatters, gleans, swirls, twists, whirls, careens and capers' all while making cutting observations about the rulers she serves and has come to pity; we hear from Emperor Babur himself in the lengthiest section, after victory at the Battle of Khanwa, fought between Babur's invading forces and the Rajput confederacy for dominion over Northern India; and finally, we hear from the Koh-i-Noor diamond, one of the largest cut diamonds in the world (weighing 105.6 carats) and once part of seventeenth-century Mughal ruler Shah Jahan's gemstone-encrusted throne (lodged at the very top in the head of a glittering peacock, and after the annexation of the Punjab in 1849, acquired by the British and placed among the crown jewels of Queen Victoria, where it still resides).

Thakore's *Mughal Sequence* is audacious, multichromatic, sui generis and conceived on the scale of Hart Crane's *Voyages* or Dylan Thomas's *Fern Hill;* were it to have been the only book of poems he ever published, it would still help cement his place in the canon. The shifts from section to section in gender, class, caste, religion and then finally materiality itself are dazzling to see attempted, let alone actually pulled off. The lexicon of the dancing girl is feminine and rhythmic—'the quivering of a drumskin, / The hall, the floor, the dance'—whereas Emperor Babur broods in paranoia, seeing 'the lips of the Shah of Persia, smiling, / As he sips his wine from his neighbour's skull' and entreating 'the benign, compassionate, all-mothering Angel of Majoon'. These are voices for the stage, orchestrated with diligent care to tell the untold history of the Mughal rulers, and the move at the end of the sequence to use the anthropomorphized voice of 'pure mineral, neither mortal nor ghost' astounds and delights. To end the sequence, the Koh-i-Noor diamond pleads:

I, who have never cared to be a seer,
Have seen these things,

And ask only now,
To be sheltered from the light that can never be mine.

Return me to the mines.
Carry me back to the dark that scorned me.

'Mughal Sequence' is as fully realized as a long poem can be. Throughout the rest of *In Praise of Bone*, there are other virtuoso constructions as well, showing Thakore's encyclopedic knowledge of poetic form. He has written nocturnes and aubades, villanelles and sonnets, odes and dramatic monologues, apostrophes and ekphrastic poems, hymns and blues, yet, there is a through line of a mind actively interrogating itself and experience in time and music, varying the tempo and tone depending on the occasion.

For instance, sometimes a whip-smart sardonic riposte is called for, such as in the gleefully wicked conclusion of 'Words to an Aspiring Surrealist':

You have good reason, perhaps, to somnambulate
In sonorous oblivion past the self you hate—
Yet what the dark brings to light may not wait

Till you outlive your delight in danger.
What is likely to last does more than linger,
And the bones of verse, my friend, are stronger

Than the half-burnt nerves of speech peeled bare,
Or that vague final image which is never quite there;
Your verse, like you, needs looking after—take care.

At other times, the humour turns subtler and more satirical as in the final quatrain of the villanelle 'Vacillations of a Recondite Nudist':

Though swans wear nothing when they break into flight—
For who can endure the slow letting go?—
Swaddled in white quilts and buttoned up tight.
I will not sleep in the nude tonight.

The distance between these pieces and the carefully constructed persona in 'Mughal Sequence' is vast and yet, tracks together salubriously and symbiotically, for there's always at root a distinctively Thakore trait of lingering in the intensity of the emotion, be it grief or laughter or outrage and shaping it with care, so that there's an integrity to the line and a necessity about the movement, whether refracted through the work of art or a historical reconstruction. 'The bones of verse', it turns out, are indeed much stronger than 'the half-burnt nerves of speech peeled bare'.

Spanning over three decades, Anand Thakore's *In Praise of Bone* is a significant poetic achievement. Permeated with a deep seeking that doesn't preclude self-loathing and regret, but that also commemorates moments of genuine pleasure and connection, often in meticulous yet organic form, the poems in this collection constitute a serious philosophical inquiry into the nature of self and how our encounters with the past, in the shape of text or image or memory or dream, help provide a scaffolding with which to climb into the present moment and experience it most fully. Fulfilling Pope's notion of being darkly wise and rudely great, Thakore is a genuine poet and many of these poems stand a fighting chance of surviving the ravages of time that are always closing in on the margins. The certainty of bone lies some uncertain distance ahead of us, but if we can learn to accept our experiences without judgement and with equanimity, we can begin to praise this transient vibration of awareness in song. We may even come to praise bone itself. Certainly, we can praise Anand Thakore's considerable poetic achievement which spurs us into discovering these connections for ourselves. *In Praise of Bone* firmly establishes Thakore as one of the finest English-language poets working in India today.

—Dr Ravi Shankar
Pushcart Prize-winning author of *Correctional*

Author's Note

For all that may be said or sung in praise of inhabiting the present moment, the process of putting together a selection of one's verse, gleaned from three decades, remains inseparable from the darkest forms of retrospection. I have often asked myself, during the course of this process, what Prospero asks his daughter in Act I of *The Tempest*:

What see'st thou else
In the dark backward and abysm of time?

And I must confess I have seen little in that abysm that has seemed, in any broader sense, worthy of preservation; though there have been events that have seemed of intense personal relevance to me, and some of these have been emergences in language: the genesis of poems.

The sections of this book are arranged in reverse chronological order: my most recent work placed first, my earliest last. 'New Poems (2015–21)' is followed by gleanings from *Seven Deaths and Four Scrolls* (2017), the entire length of *Mughal Sequence* (2012) and selected pieces from *Elephant Bathing* (2012) and *Waking in December* (2001). The title of this collection is identical to that of a poem I wrote at twenty-three. I could, admittedly, have been more inventive, and racked my brains till I stumbled upon a new title; but it struck me suddenly that at the core of my lyrical attempts, there lay at once a need to celebrate the subliminal structures of things and a fascination with death—both themes that the word 'bone' seemed to naturally embrace.

Somewhere in my late teens or early twenties, I had begun to seriously consider the possibility of a poetics that aligned itself with my parallel concerns as a student and performer of Hindustani vocal music; a possibility, which I believed, could be realised through a symbiosis between musical and literary forms, and which involved, necessarily, a bridging of gaps between mediums and cultures. When I wrote the short poem that lends this book its name, I was studying for an MA in English Literature at the University of Poona, while also receiving guidance in the theory and practice of Hindustani music from Pandit Satyasheel Deshpande. I had, at the time, received a scholarship from The Ministry of Human Resource Development to help me pursue my musical endeavours and musical performance was soon to become my primary career. Over the years, there have been phases during which I have found my musical and literary processes inseparably intertwined; others during which I have grown sceptical about their apparent interdependence.

My first two books seem obsessively concerned with the need to push speech in the direction of song; to seek out in words the varied benedictions of a 'higher' musical order. But I can now discern in my poetic strategies a growing counter-obsession that ran parallel to this: an obsession with speech per se; and a concomitant need to concentrate my energies in verse on what began to seem possible to me only in verbal language.

The next two collections, *Mughal Sequence* and *Seven Deaths and Four Scrolls*, involve a different set of principles from those on which my previous work was based. Both books are sequences of dramatic monologues welded together by an underlying sense of unity at the level of theme and form. *Mughal Sequence* seeks unity in historical specificity; *Seven Deaths and Four Scrolls*, in the expansive but ultimately unifying theme of death. Both sequences attempt to accommodate individual poems within the framework of a bigger structure, a broader scheme of things—an approach to art I seem to trust in less, the longer I live and write.

In my more recent work—much of which emerged in response to the sudden demise of childhood friend and fellow-poet Deepankar Khiwani—I have sought to return (sometimes unsuccessfully, perhaps) to what I like to call an 'each-poem-for-itself' approach. I had begun to sense the dangers inherent in a method that repeatedly pushed poetry towards drama and narrative prose; and this was followed by a sense of relief in no longer needing to contain specific poems within wider constructs. That sense of relief has much to do, I believe, with a heightened willingness to embrace the immediate; and if age and poetry are now teaching me to do that, I am grateful.

New Poems

(2015–2021)

Obverse

Because you will never see this I now write this line:
the image on my mobile screen—
one side of a face
on a coin from the age of Constantine the Great;
the wreathed head and sinister single eye
of a man whom—of course—
no-one alive could possibly have seen.

A Coin for the boatman, Anand?—I'm well beyond that now…

Hmm…a retort, as expected! I sense your wit, my friend,
your boyhood love of the Hellenic—but no, I remind myself,
this isn't *you* speaking,
just me mumbling to myself the sort of thing
you *might* have said.
I want to show you this coin,
this printed face in profile,
though it seems unlikely—even if I could—
that where you now are
such things continue to interest you:

you, who always said I could never quite see you,
because I never paused long enough to look;
because each time your eyes were about to say something
your lips couldn't say, I looked aside.
I want you to know:
it is because you will never see them
I now write these lines.

Dawn at Lake Pangong

Waking to grope through peak, lake and sky
For signs of some release beyond the mind's
Power to grant, he seeks to set the eye
Adrift at dawn upon a ripple—yet finds,

As he strains his gaze to trace without a blink
Those widening curves and their shifting glint,
A lifetime of failure stalks him to the brink.
He brings to those blues the frozen black of print,

And finds the clearest waters his eyes have seen,
Cluttered by words he cannot now unsay.
No force within his grasp can now wipe clean

What spreads like ink as he shuts his eyes to pray—
The blackness of words outlived yet here to stay,
Afloat like dirt upon the lake's blue sheen.

Joseph and Potiphar's Wife

for Deepankar Khiwani, author of
'Portrait of the Artist as a Middle-Aged Woman'

Solihull School, February, nineteen eighty-two.
Seen against a backdrop of wiry trees
And sheets of snow, a frozen quadrangle,
A football field frosted over, our Scripture teacher
Mrs H., in thermal slacks and unusually high heels,
Looks more desirable than ever, as she instructs her flock

Of fidgety eleven-year-olds, just back from Christmas-break,
To depict in crayon and pencil, a scene from the life of Joseph.
Enslavement and *the-coat-of-many-colours*
Suggest themselves at once as obvious themes,
Amongst brief thoughts concerning bakers and grapes;
But something about my Scripture teacher's ineffable rump

Calls to mind the tale of Joseph and Potiphar's wife.
I put down my colour-pencils and take a deep breath,
Before slipping into my private, contorted version of the tale,
According to which the two protagonists, having made love
Many times over, finally get caught in the act,
And Mrs Potiphar cries rape in utter defencelessness,

To save herself from being thrown to the crocodiles.
I shut my eyes and play at being either of them in turn:
Now I am Joseph—not lurching back, startled by an
Impassioned tug at his loincloth, as our *Children's Illustrated Bible*
Portrays him, his palms retracted in sanctimonious refusal,
But feasting instead to the utmost upon her lips and breasts;

And now I am *her*, serpentine, venomous,
My breasts slipping out from the papyrus-like coils
Of the same silver gown our Children's Bible conceals hers in,
My lips pressed firm round his startling member,
Awaiting in ecstatic ignorance some savage enigmatic thrust,
Some cryptic overflow that I imagine as I may

But as yet possess no clear knowledge of,
Bare dunes and muralled walls swinging,
Amidst pulsating hieroglyphs and slavish salivations,
Round pillars rocking, till the Nile
And all the pyramids consign themselves to darkness,
And all Egypt falls asleep to the sound of our moaning.

Outside, beyond the double-glazed windows,
Tall men in black scatter salt on ice. Here,
In Scripture-class, laid out on shelves above the coils
Of classroom heaters, as I stare, amidst premonitions
Of an unfathomable heat, at a blank notebook page,
Wet rows of tiny, fingerless gloves thaw and drip.

Waterhole

Something in the blood wants to leap,
Here, outside the ICU my father's in,
His speech now taken from him,

By bandages, tubes and pipes.
What wants to leap is like the sound and stroke
Of a bright steel plectrum against a taut tuned string,

The hollow russet gourd with its bridge of horn,
Leaf-decked and lacquered in Calcutta in his early teens,
Reverberating with the tiles of a mosaic floor,

Laid down at his grandfather's behest to allure the dead—
An untameable sound, febrile, metallic,
That reaches out not for perfection of pitch or form,

But for the undergrowth of forests visited in solitude,
Between sessions at court or five-star hotels.
It is a music that summons the jungle home,

Beseeching it to inhabit the domain of time-hallowed metres,
And arched, ancestral walls, once believed indomitable;
Each creepered phrase, each verdurous pause,

Urging it to confer, on territories of tone
That have stood like temples,
Its uncontrollable strength.

What longs to leap is impassioned
As the sound of strings he tuned and strummed,
Pulled, plucked and put aside for years;

But also, it is as tuneless, aloof and swift,
As the single click of a black-and-white camera,
Heard, against the torrid crunch

Of desiccated leaf-beds crumpled by hooves,
Amidst crane-squawk, deer-bark, cricket-hum and monkey-screech,
In the parched interior of a landlocked forest

Towards the end of March,
When trees turn skeletal, and all streams for miles around
Run dry, all pools but this one—

His breath slowing down,
As he turns from the lens to the thought of thirst,
And rows of antlers sail cautiously into view,

Till it is time to gather with those who have gathered,
Receiving what deer and buffalo receive,
Asking to live, here only for water.

Threesome

So now you call long-distance to remind me
My late friend is not just mine to mourn,
But also *yours*—
Though things turned sour between you,
And the two of you haven't spoken in twenty years.
I understand: you wish to reclaim a lost right to grief,
And to tell me—though, of course, you do not mention this—
That in the great list of things we have shared, you and I—
Tarkovsky, Tolkien, riverfish in mustard sauce,
Boat rides, skinny-dipping, rain,
The same therapist, the same cheap rooms in gimcrack hotels—
We must not now forget to include
A dead man's insatiable, irretrievable member.
You will want to fondle them, perhaps,
When you read this, alone in your room
On your laptop screen with the lights switched off,
The breasts I could never quite bring myself to share—
Though I tried, believe me—
With the recently dead.

On Reading Richard II a Second Time

So is it in the music of men's lives…
—Shakespeare, *Richard II*

Is it because you will never now hear
The things I still have left to say,
That I begin to hear this?

—Sense and cadence of a pair of lines,
Once glanced at and passed by
Without so much as a pause—

Your absence alerts me to a music I was deaf to,
Teaching me to linger
Upon the cold stone slabs of a prison cell
Where a man who once wore a crown
Is about to be murdered.

I want you to hear him cry for silence,
Fearing the sound of a string will drive him mad.

That's How It Feels

You claimed you preferred the safety of public spaces;
To appear at bookstores, a park, a hotel pool.
I had grown attuned to your frequent assaults on sleep;
Till late last night you chose to blast the rule,

And accost me in a room where only you could see me.
Your eyes held mine with a stare hell-bent on slaughter.
I recall a feverish ripping of shirts, the pressure
Of nails on astonished skin, but little thereafter,

Except the sound of the flesh crying out for more.
When you bit my lips I'm certain they bled.
You loosened your grip, then rose and reached for the door.

A salt-lamp quivered in the dark. *There,* you said,
I told you one day you'd get what you've always longed for:
That's how it feels to get fucked awake by the dead.

Sea Link

A swerve to the left and at last I can see from outside
The city I was raised in: at the edge of the village on my right,
A finger of rock laid bare by an ebbing tide,
The skyline retreating in darkness and halogen light.

Surely the voice at once spoke true and lied
That said I belong to this city of slums and towers.
There's a side of me that wants to cast aside
What links us together to commonly call it *ours*.

And bound to it in concrete this—*our very own
Brand new Sea Link*—remains inseverable from what I love
And long to flee; though it claims to stand alone.

Here none may linger; all must always move.
It isn't true, but there's relief in pretending one
Is through, as taut white cables fly backwards above.

Nocturne at Afghan Church[*]

Raised in remembrance of a war that could never be won,
Poised in silence against the dark they stand:
Spire and lamplit arch conspiring to sing
How the tongue I now speak took root in this land

Of mangoes, mangroves, lianas and incessant heat.
How sharp against the night their silence rings true—
Syllables of stone that praise a resplendent defeat,
And the triumph of a language no tongue may subdue;

Whose defiant consonants and inscrutable cadence,
Victor and vanquished alike shall never rein in—
Syllables of stone that grow in silence immense,
And presage our return to that emptiness wherein
Our efforts at speech pristinely begin;
Against the tongues we speak, we are not born to win.

---

[*]Built in Mumbai in 1858 to honour the British soldiers who died in the campaigns against Afghanistan, a territory that was never successfully annexed to the British Empire.

Brazil

When first she brought you home I must have been seven;
She who had flown in triumph half-way around you.
Now past fifty I know I have not been forgiven
For being so unlike her. The countries I have visited are few.

From the shelf where you sit Brazil stares me in the face,
Amidst wide strips of unconquered sea and land.
Surely it's no crime to stay rooted to one place!
I have moved in ways she could never understand,

Gazing at what's right here as at seas from an airplane—
And there's some comfort there…though I remain
Drawn at times to that glorious curve she drew,
Traversing with a single finger one half of you;
The circle she began and left me to complete:
Wiser by far, mother, not to compete.

Two Miniatures

I

DIWALI ON THE PALACE ROOF

Kishangarh, eighteenth century

Where the light from my reading-lamp falls on this open page
It is always Diwali night and we have nothing to do

But wait and watch while the palace concubines
Lift and wave lit sparklers to amuse us;

Watch black and gold revive old questions,
Till gold betrays its transience, yielding to black—

Each minuscule spark, frozen in paint,
Resigning itself in sudden contentment

To the knowledge of its own brevity,
Coming gently to understand

That night will have her way and must be allowed to.
Where the light from this reading lamp falls

On this open page, we begin to see
That fire is just another game night likes to play,

That this is true of each of us too,
That we are aspects of the night,

And night will have her way.

II

SUDAMA TAKES KRISHNA'S LEAVE

Chamba Valley, eighteenth century

Here colour reserves the right to hold back the future:
Raw contrast of the feather-crowned monarch's

Fine yellow robes and gold brick walls,
With the frayed grey loincloth of his departing friend,

Now turning to take his host's final leave,
Now navigating,

Homebound and out alone in the open,
Beyond sealed gates and thick, outer walls of gold,

A sparse, pathless green
Which reveals no hint of the miracle that awaits him:

The sudden undreamed-of house with its plates of gold coins,
The abundance of his courtyard, the laughter of his children,

Upon this page forever postponed.

Horse Trainer

Sketch and watercolour, Mongolian, late nineteenth century

Listen: at the heart of the desert,
Amidst the listless wastes of innermost Mongolia,
The sudden, silent thud of brush and ink.

Hoofprints on dunes, hoofbeats on paper,
A sinuous tide of horses outleaping paper,
A frothing, furious surge of outflung necks and manes

That only the whip and call
Of the mounted man in green may rule and restrain,
As he surfs on thunderous waves of horsehair.

Your voice is a cunning moon, horselord,
That holds back the tides your whip drives on;
All gallops at your will and is held in place,

All bends to the will of your lyrical horsecraft.

Man and Woman Gazing at the Moon

Friedrich, c.1830

Something about these autumnal branches,
And sinuous roots heaped with moss;

Or the blurred, distant green of pines
Drooping at the edge of a ridge,

Now renews in the eye
A tenuous reverence for lavender evenings.

To look on from here,
Is to know one must remain outside,

Acquiescing to the unknowable,
Conceding to the power of the unalterably unseen:

Man and woman gazing at the moon—
Their faces, because never painted, forever invisible—

Here seen from behind as nothing more
Than a wide black cloak and hat, a tenebrous gown,

Green yielding to strains of salmon-pink and purple,
The moss beneath thickening.

Standing Stone Saraswati, Twelfth Century, Deccan

Victim of a faith that will never understand her,
>   Defaced, mastectomised, her many arms mutilated,
Then left to lie at the bottom of a pond for centuries,

She is now object who once was divine—
>   Her face flattened featureless,
Her stone lute lost, her right leg a cleft,

Bare ridges of quarried rock where garlanded breasts
>   Once brazenly hung.
No sign remains here now, upon the cratered waist and torso,

Or amidst these tides of bruised rock, round chunks of shoulder,
>   Shards of a bracelet, shreds of an elaborate girdle,
To remind us that this indeed is she: white-robed matriarch,

Virgin, patroness and progenitor of all speech and song.
>   Now only the peacock at her feet survives intact,
To tell us afresh of her erstwhile power,

Its form complete, its frame unharmed from crest to tail,
>   Its open beak and intricately detailed plumage
Believed perhaps—unlike the lost features and breasts

Of the goddess herself—neither heathen nor offensive enough,
>   To merit the marauder's triumphant tribal rage;
The little claws and long tail, the proud feathered chest

And slender upturned neck,
>   No serious threat to the invader's abstract monolithic order,
Unworthy of his victorious, descending axe.

Constantinople, 1453

I

ANGELUS OF A BYZANTINE COURTESAN

Virgin Mary have pity on us whores,
On women sequestered in your city's exquisite bordellos,
Now too famished to work. Have pity on our pimps.
The King's men hoard what little remains of our Genoese grain,
And hunger now walks through our city with the face of a Turk.
Our resilience dwindles. Our bastards starve.
A red moon rises over the Hagia Sophia,
Above the Red Apple, the Bosphorus, Galata,
Mocking our battlements, the few ships still moored in the Golden Horn;
And Venice, for sure, has now abandoned us.

Be with us through this night, lady, us vermin of the night,
And if, before morning—as they now surely will—
The virgin gates of your city should finally give way
To the pounding of battering ram and heathen cannonade,
Be still amongst us at that fall; and with those of this city
Whose stomachs still fatten on guarded wheat.
And do not abandon those women whose disdain we have borne,
Who were married in your churches.

We who were bred to feed alike
On the varied hungers of Christian and Turk—
Appeasing each according to his special needs—
Are better prepared than most for what is now to come.
You, Lady, ravished by heaven—Sentinel of stern walls—

Made fecund, as you were, through no choice of your own,
Would understand, possibly, better than most,
The peculiar fortitude of our tribe.

Be present for them when they are raped, mother,
The women who scorned us.
Be present for their sons
When they are sodomised—
Husbands, fathers, brothers brought in to watch—
Inure them in time, as we have been,
To the torment of enslavement and rape.
Instruct them, mother,
In the arts we were raised to study as children.

II

CONSTANTINE XI SEES A RED MOON RISE

> *Better to die on one's feet than live on one's knees.*
> —Lyonidas, Thermopylae

Against the speech of the sky, nothing that may be said or done
Is of any use to us now.
I foresaw this in nightmares, cautioned by strange rumours.

When I gave the command to melt down our sacred silver,
To mint new coin for my mercenaries,
I knew in a minute,
That a thousand years had come to an end,
That Venice had forgotten us, the age of crusades was over—
No fervent broadsword would now rise to turn
The tide of scimitars that lashed at our doors.

No frenzied orison rose through my veins;
Nor could I hear them complain—effigy, crucifix,
Casket and chalice, candlestand and cross,
When called upon to surrender their shapes to fire;
Unmade and moulded into slim, identical discs,
Terrifying as this moon,
Lighter than the coin of my forbears,
Yet stamped with the indelible weight of my face, my crown,
A name handed down to me by this town's great founder.

They tell me a ship awaits me in the Golden Horn,
The Lords of Byzantium, now anxious to leave.
Set sail, my lords, with my goodwill,
While safe passage remains a possibility.
As for me—though History may add me
To its list of martyrs,
Applauding my unwillingness to embark—
Neither faith nor glory nor love of homeland
Are what keep me here.
I linger because I am sick of survival,
This restless business of staying alive.

What shall I make of your words, Lyonidas?
All vain speech, perhaps, against the speech of this moon!
I, Constantine, eleventh of that name,
Have no wish to live, either on my feet or on my knees…
Though your ancient rhetoric might prove useful,
When I rally my men at daybreak;
As also, Lady of Our City, your immaculate name.

Stay with us, Lady, at that charge,
Though you know it is not for your sake I dream
Of throwing myself where the lines throng thickest.
Be with my mercenaries when they desert our turrets
And hurry to the harbour.
Clasp me as I fall—
And let the last ship sail.

Nuptials at Somaiya House

Black and white enlarged, Walkeshvar Road, Mumbai 1934

I

EPITHALAMION

Between two towers of freshly painted pots,
Held firm, beneath long garlands of marigold and mango leaf,
By lengths of bamboo and banana stems,
Grim centuries of frozen prejudice thaw in these flames.

The priests on either side of bride and groom,
Stare statuesque, like everyone else,
At a lens that requires them to sit still for five minutes.
There is silence here, after long hours of chanting,

Slow evenings of courtship in senior college alcoves,
And months of loud slogans flung through prison bars
At anglophone wardens and local policemen
In protest against the crown.

My grandmother's father looks on with pride
At the symbolic dissolution of a hate more ancient
Than the reams of metered Sanskrit incanted above this fire,
His daughter received into no home

But the one she was born and grew up in:
Somaiya House, overlooking the sea,
Its courtyard decked with festoons of mogra.
The man who sits on the carpet beside her,

Who will read *Lamb's Tales* to me, when I am eight or nine,
And fold palms at her bedside as she fades at ninety—
Let it happen quickly, lord, we are grateful for death—
Sports the coarsest homespun cotton cloth:

High-born fugitive of Brahma-Kshatriya descent,
Outlawed by his clan, cast out by his parents
For marrying a woman of the merchant caste—
Their absence from the frame, eight decades from this moment,

Now marked in dawnlight with unsought forgiveness.

II

NO PLACE FOR WOMEN

Wilson College, nineteen-thirty:
My grandmother has failed her Philosophy exams,
And will spend the rest of her life wondering
Why she chose the subject instead of Literature,

Her failure a confirmation in her mother's eyes
Of the notion that college is no place for women.
The man she will marry tries to console her
By misquoting Wordsworth at his worst,

In second person and present tense:
You are a phantom—etcetera...
Lines he will come to acquaint me with—
In their original form, thankfully—

As I reach my teens, the last verse of the piece
By then of heightened personal relevance to him.
From beneath the rounded arches they look out at a sea,
They will never care to cross by boat or plane,

Content never to depart from the soil
Their tribe now strives to claim for its own.
Prison will part them. Allowed only so many sheets
In a month, he will write to her in the tiniest handwriting,

On scraps of paper his soap comes wrapped in,
Implore a friendly jailor to smuggle them out.
Together for now, Tilak and Gandhi ringing in their ears,
Their hearts strengthened by strains of Tagore

And Jhaverchand Meghani, against all they must oppose for love,
The nation they envision looking up from these alcoves
Is one whose existence can only be unreal.
—*Have we nothing but our dreams?*

—*The sea, my sweetheart, look at the sea…*
—*And what if freedom is a lie?*
—*O look, Kapila, my darling, it's raining.*
Across the sea, across a desert and two continents, England,

Whose poets they praise and whose policies they oppose,
Will persist as she has,
While the nation they look up to from beneath these arches,
Withers with their vision till it turns ghost-pale,

A myth the bones find harder to believe in
As they weaken with time:
—*This is not what we laboured for surely…*
—*But there has been progress, Kapila, progress.*

—*Ekaj de chingaari mahaanal*—all I ask of the fire
At the core of all things, is a single spark—
But why Philosophy? —she will blurt out over meals
In the weeks before her death—*forget me*, her motto,

Having authored over thirty books for children in Gujarati,
And translated several of her favourite novels from English—
What else can it possibly be but a great waste of time,
Confusion for no good reason?

Never really cared to understand it, not a word.

III

SOMAIYA HOUSE

What ghosts frequent Somaiya House I cannot say:
A whole grey tribe of grand-uncles and aunts, perhaps,
Still groping for a nation that is never quite born;
A great-grandfather who was mayor of Mumbai—which is

What he would have called it, in his time, in Gujarati;
A grand-aunt who never married,
Who earned a living teaching collegian girls
How to drive—and loved to talk at length

About all the suitors she had rejected in her youth.
Perhaps the ancestral dead return as they lived—groping;
Though I prefer to believe they come, if at all they do,
To free themselves at last of the dreams they lived for,

Relinquishing these decrepit floors and walls,
These rotten doors that lead to their most cherished haunts—
The cracked stone slabs and wrought-iron spiral stair,
The castle-thick arches and wooden floorboards

Of Somaiya House, once home to so many who chose
Incarceration as a means to freedom,
Now abandoned by the living, sold to a builder
And scheduled for demolition, its empty balconies

Still looking towards England, facing the sea.

Thamyris

> *Because he proudly durst affirm he could more sweetly sing…*
> —*Chapman's Homer's Iliad*, Book II

Now paralysed by gods he was favoured by and sought to surpass,
His fingers, once adept, still grope to strike those strings
That stirred the most impervious of men to tears,
Hauling their souls skywards on thunderous wings.

Will Hades revive that praise of an imagined order, that fraud
Of the mortal heart or divine deceit that makes men sing?
Here, amongst the living, there is order in nothing;
No fervent continuum, no furtive humming

Persists beneath the shattered surfaces of things.
Those hills and resonant valleys, woods and island-caves
He wove his songs in, stand stripped of their echoes. His hands
Are rocks. His ears close round him like a pair of graves,

And the waves of the Aegean are made of lead.
A crass cacophony drowns their prayerful refrain.
No tunes now leap from the throats of the remembered dead.
No cadence turns to greet his toneless pain—

Celebrant of the moonstruck shoreline, songster of the self,
Whose thrust in a single flash could so easily disperse
All thoughts that darkened and fettered the widening heart—
Who summoned in speech the Muses' curse,

And a guilt that all who live by song must share,
Longing to believe himself sole claimant and source
Of a gift only partly his own, if at all—his voice
Now sealed in a void, drained by the fates of all former force.

Basic Winemaking for Beginners,

by Brian Leverett, if I'm not mistaken,
was the name of the book I chanced upon at eighteen,
at the streetside bookstore near Flora Fountain.

Sometimes I miss the boy,
who combed the back-alleys behind Crawford Market,
for what chapter one referred to as *essential equipment*:
a glass Hydrometer with a measuring cylinder,
a length of thin, plastic pipe;
a five-litre demijohn with an airlock
and a one-hole rubber stopper
of precisely the right size
to fit and choke its mouth.

The boy who searched those streets
is trying to show me what it takes
to pick out the darkest sultanas in a dry-fruits store,
and prevent any bitterness
in the imminent wine
by stripping five oranges
of their pips and pith—
he is trying to show me how to cast
like a spell upon the must a fistful of yeast
and feel it frothing there for three days
with little space to breathe—
taking care to stir and air it out once in a day.—
And he wants me to recall how it feels
to strain all that blood for the first time
through a thin white sieve,
watching it drip into an air-tight jar

that allows it to exhale
but never breathe in.
Now come the months of waiting,
of listening to the nascent wine—
like pressing an ear against a womb
to hear a foetus kicking there on the verge of birth—
the effervescence dying down
with that slow death of yeast
till a thick haze clears
and all that frenzied bubbling is heard no more.
Time now to harvest and siphon out into bottles
all this blood, now transparent—
gently, so as not to disturb the deceased
settled like sand at the bottom of a lake.
Pipes, corks…and then more weeks of waiting
till suddenly it is time
to lift to the light and taste his first full glass
of home-made orange-sultana wine: now,
approaching fifty, the boy who searched those streets
is learning what it takes,
to lift to the light an invisible glass,
filled to the brim with a brew
it is not for *him* to taste;
what it means to stare *through* its clear pink,
breathe *in* its fragrance.

Ringtone

Somewhere outside a classroom in an Eng. Lit. Department
A woman I have never seen before
Is about to appear and correct my French.

Strange way to fall in love:
Conceding with a glance that your French is better than mine!—
Admitting—without words, of course—that a sentence
Blurted out in French by a count or his valet
In an English translation of *War and Peace*
Doesn't quite mean what I just *said* it means.

Now thirty years since I watched a thin bookmark sail to the floor
And shut an old novel midway to begin my studies of *you*.
We now all have—in place of the uniform, universalised
Double-tring of landlines—our own selectively personalised
Ringtones to await and answer;
And I've been whispering things to myself all evening,
Giving in to the old mistake of believing
That anything I say means what I think it means.

Appear unsummoned, Love.
Call me before I call you tonight.
I linger and stare at the wallpaper on my cell-phone,
Sitting back by the window, waiting to stand corrected.

Evidence

The evidence of God's existence has got up early this morning.
(I know this for a fact because she messaged me at dawn
To tell me she was about to feed the chickens in the yard.)
There's a telescope, I've heard, on Mauna Kea in Hawaii
That can detect a candle flame on the moon.
I'm the son of a lawyer who studied Physics in his youth;
And my skills at examining the evidence
Have been improving of late.
(I can even detect, at times, across six thousand miles,
The beginnings of a smile.)
The evidence—of course—still refuses to believe
In the facts it was set before me to prove.
It wants me to know where I sit past midnight,
How hard it is trying just now to trust its own hands—
And with how little success—
Squirming through dawnlight, scattering corn.

Hymns of a Broken Man

I

WATERSNAKE

What I have poisoned will be cleansed;
I am what is cleansed and he who poisons—

But now: joy of defeat at the hands of one
Who was me before I knew it, before I was.

O Silence my concubines,
Be deaf to their anxious hisses for mercy,

For I am your dance floor—
And would perish knowing this.

Now bind my several heads into a single music.

II

MATINS

Ride this mad tiger, lady, subdue him, quick.
Let him not claw himself,

Or rip his own flesh with his swift incisors.
Lighten his load by becoming his sole burden,

And swallow his trump card before he plays it again—
Overbold survivor, incorrigible victim,

Baring with his teeth trite histories of abuse,
As he pulls to old wounds imaginary crowds.

Goad him with the blunt end of your trident;
Bring him to the cat-flap that has so often saved him,

And let him shrink there in the light of your lifted right palm,
The old roar lowering to the pitch of a purr,

Till he squeezes his way into your most gracious kitchen.
Then come to him, lady, where he sits,

Hiding his face with his paws, mewing for your touch,
Crouched in the closet beneath the sink—

Little shivering Siamese,
Last living kitten of an unsalvageable litter—

Run your fingers through his fur, lady,
Where all notions desert him and his demons await you.

III

VIEW FROM A SHIVA SHRINE

Hanging Gardens, Mumbai

Seen from this distance, through the last hillside thicket
Left upon the island, now for a moment

On the other side of beach and bay, this seething city—
Its endless skyscrapers veiled behind foliage,

Its relentless car-horns muted by the height—
Grows suddenly so much easier to befriend.

Here distance asserts its ancient equation:
To sing in praise of where I am

Is to praise the distance at which cities seem forgiven
On evenings like these at the ringing of a bell

Their infinite cruelties and unyielding ways.
I praise the distance at which cities are forgiven.

Two Poems Borrowed from the Saints

for Arundhathi Subramaniam

I

THE NAME

after Tulsidas, doha, Ramacharitamanas, Adikanda

The name of Rama is a universal tree
That shelters us in these fallen times—

And merely recalling it has taught me
To be true to my own:

For I, Tulsidas, who was scrawny and dry
As a leaf of cannabis,

Have now turned as green and life-giving,
As a leaf of the tulsi-plant;

The name of Rama has brought me to delight in my own.

II

THE FLUTE

after Surdas, 'Murali Adhar Saji Balbeer'

The flute has but to touch his lips and see—

Women run wild at the sound, out into the forest,
Forgetting to take their garments with them—

The flute has but to touch his lips.

A cow looks up from her grazing,
Her calf lets go of her nipples,

The flute has but to touch his lips,

And a bird shuts his eyes to listen,
Quiet as a seer in deepest contemplation.

Neither creeper nor grass quiver now,
Though a light, scented breeze blows between them;

Now even the Jamuna, Surdas, wants to slow down,
Stay back and listen. See: her waters retreat.

The flute has but to touch his lips.

Variation for Buddha Purnima

For losing rhythm while accompanying a dancing apsara in the court of Indra, a gandharva is cursed by the King of the Gods. As penance, he must spend 3,000 years upon the earth in human form, awaiting his hour of redemption. Around 480 BC, he seeks employment as a music teacher at the court of Shudhodhana, King of the Shakhyas in Nepal.

His father assured me he would pay me well
so long as I promised him in return,
to acquaint his son
only with the most erotic of compositions,
the most sensual themes,
keeping devotion, as such—
not to mention 'other-worldliness'—entirely at bay.
I wanted to explain to him that this was hardly possible—
but then, agreed to his terms:
after all, life at court—
though a far cry from heaven—
is just about as pleasant as it gets round here;
and I, who am bound to pay
with three thousand years of mortality,
the price of a single missed beat,
must now receive with grace what comes my way.
Come to me, boy.
There have been things said about you at your birth
that make me tremble to teach you how to tune a string…
(though there is something about you—not talent certainly,
I can recognise *that*—
which suggests an unforeseen delight in being human.)
The wooden pegs, boy…this is how you do it,
a lightening of the breath before you tighten the strings.

Lines to my Secret Mentor
with a Verse by Emerson

> *The ancient symbols will be nothing then,*
> *We shall have gone behind the symbols*
> *To that which they symbolised…*
> —Wallace Stevens, 'The Sail of Ulysses'

If you are the hymn the Brahmin sings,
Tighten my pyjama-strings.

Lift this low whimper to the pitch of a shout,
Or with the old gesture mute it out.

My song that shone like a sword now gropes for a sheath;
Its burgeoning vowels run short of breath,

Its consonants fall like worn-out teeth,
Its metres collapse at the thought of death,

As my hands turn back from dangling ends in fear,
And I turn as limp as these trousers I wear.

O grant this sinking cadence the levity of hyacinths;
Resuscitate its floundering middle C, its decentred sevenths.

Salvage these timorous inflections from imaginary eyes,
Whose faithless cravings now urge them to sermonise.

Grant them new firmness in the face of old terror,
Of the mirror's familiar plots, the primeval error

Of needing to be understood by anyone but you.
Let the heart contain them. Let them brew—

And if, as you say, when you I fly, you are the wings,
Acquaint them with the furtive semiotics of pyjama-strings.

Let none comprehend us and the singing be strong—
O lave me with the lore of the unstruck gong!

And string my defeated quavers into rosaries of sound,
Till this whole foretold sentence comes gently round,

Where *you* now place it. Now, while pride
Still seems a prerogative of the crude,

While the nerves relinquish their ancestral claim
To all knowledge of tone or tune or form or time;

And thought sits useless as a broken pot—
Bind, before I believe the great books lie,

The ineffably simple, self-redeeming knot
I cannot bring my tired hands to tie.

Set me with a jolt upon the journey out—
For You are the doubter and the doubt,

And You are the hymn the Brahmin sings,
And You are the lord of pyjama-strings.

From *Seven Deaths and Four Scrolls*

(2017)

'Puppet's Life Ends on String'

The lone surviving gunman of 26/11 was hanged at Pune's Yerawada Jail at 7.30 a.m. on Wednesday. Asked for his last wish the twenty-five-year-old terrorist from Faridkot village in Pakistan's Punjab province said, 'Gharwalon ko milna hai' (I want to meet my family).

—The Times of India, 22 November, 2012

See: they recur, approach and recur beyond terror and grave,
The low tin roofs and ambient wheat fields,
The hills and goat-filled alleys of remembered infancy—

And soon—but here they are already,
Filling their water-pots, tending to their goats,
Those I could not forgive for being so poor,

So blind to my rage; for refusing
To see themselves reflected in my hate.
They cannot see me now, of course,

Capering through barbed wire and thin mud walls—
But this is hardly strange;
It was so much like this when I lived amongst them,

Only suddenly more acceptable now.
What is strange is being unable to feel the cold they feel,
The fireside warmth, as winter comes over us

Here in Faridkot, village of my birth, visited once
And blessed for all time—as my mother
Never forgot to mention at meals—by the Sufi,

Baba Farid, mystic of the floating basket,
Whose rapt levitations I marvelled at as a child,
And whose spirit I spat upon when I turned fourteen:

There was so little left by then in our lives to praise,
And his talk of delight in poverty had come to seem
Like senseless rant; the little land we owned sold

For so little, our torn pockets empty, our jackets threadbare,
As we stared, half-starved, at the last full moon before Id,
With no goats left to fatten and slaughter, or barter for new clothes

And sweets; no money for cooking-oil or kerosene, then none
For wheat; and then, to top it all, that hard, unoutstareable look
In the eyes of a tribal girl, which could only mean no, never,

Not good enough, never will be—Baba Farid,
Whom I dismissed as a fake when I turned into a man,
And whose verse the living still lift their arms to,

In the warmth of winter fires at Faridkot!
I am glad he was with me,
Before that final steeling of burnt nerves against all fear—

Terror of the torqued neck, trapdoor and noose—
Your last wish, he said, will not be granted,
But will surely be voiced—

A single sentence that survives your death.
I am glad it was this and nothing else:
Let them come to me now—listen, I say it again—

Those I ran away from; *gharwalon ko milna hai.*

'Buddhist Monk Hangs Self'

A twenty-four-year-old Buddhist monk committed suicide at the Mahabodhi Society in Egmore, Chennai, on Sunday. Police said the monk did not leave any suicide note but had written in his diary that he wanted to find peace of mind. He was to catch a train to Bodh Gaya, Bihar, on Monday morning.

—The New Indian Express, 7 January, 2013

SCROLL ONE

The hills of Ladakh, should I ever return there,
Will not echo my speech as they used to,
When I hollered up their cliffs as a boy of thirteen,

My vowels bound skywards, or lingering in clefts,
Till glaciers returned them to the valley below.
My kinsfolk in the village will be unable to hear me,

And I have ceased to wish it otherwise.
I have been brought where I am to put them behind me;
Though here, in the hard hiatus,

The sharp, irreversible reprieve between birth and birth,
Caught in this blizzard of images that spin like prayer-wheels—
Late shadows of mountains, the valley sunless,

Smell of sweat and incense, honey and sundried venison,
Yoghurt in an earthen pot, an infant's fingers groping
For the feel of a shawl hanging from a nail—here,

Amidst blown scraps of a partly remembered life—
Hoofprints of ponies on unscalable glaciers,
Then rail-tracks, and the gaping, cadaverous lips of mountain-tunnels,

Grey leagues of highway, the dominion of traffic lights,
And a sudden anxiety, about whether all stations remain
Exactly where we leave them,

As clouds of exhaust and cement dust assail us
In the inhabited underbelly of an unfinished overpass,
Past acres of slum, grim acres of weak tin

And corrugated cement streaked with blue plastic
To keep out rain—here, amidst the stench,
Fumes, crowds, towers and endless smoke,

The unyielding car-horns and juddering motors
Of sudden, desirable cites,
That lured the heart and choked the throat,

My veins clogged with too many thoughts,
Like traffic-ridden streets beneath new flyovers—
And amidst so much I thought myself unhampered by:

The endlessly revolving doors of a vast new shopping mall
Somewhere on the road to Egmore perhaps,
Its windows festooned at Christmas

With iridescent rows of jeans and T-shirts,
That had seemed so humble
When I compared them to my own brown robes;

And all those gadgets—iPads, iPods, laptops and television sets,
Which in the flesh I did not know I secretly craved,
Yet now still cling to what's left of me—

Here, amidst all I must let go of to move ahead,
With the drone of young rivers and the smell of yak-fur,
The first faces recur, like audible fragments

Of a chant one assumes unbroken.
I sense in their gaze the hurt I caused them,
And the unaltered presence of parental will;

Yet cannot tell if it is me they are looking for,
As they wade through snowdrifts on avalanched paths,
Or look up from mule-tracks on jagged crags,

Strapped to their loss, their fingers chapped
By ropes and reins and winter, their eyes heavy as hillside rocks,
Weighed down by regret for some unguessed mistake.

There remains, on my part, the searing presence
Of so much I could hold myself accountable for—but no,
I did not choose a life that denies the flesh,

The cheerless fellowship of the sash and shaven head,
The life of the rosary, robe and silent room,
Any more than I chose the hand I died by.

That choice was theirs, for a child born,
As the whole tribe agreed, with the right signs for monkhood,
The right shape of skull, his arms the right length,

His life's purpose a given, a birthday present from a withering race
Whose ways are now not likely to survive.
That choice was theirs—yet only so much theirs

As the carcass I stepped out of might be said to be mine,
As names may be said to belong to the deceased,
Homelands to the exiled, dreams to the living,

Futures to those who remain unborn;
So much and no more—
Though it is only here perhaps,

Between birth and birth, that one begins to admit this,
Accept, that to be born is to be possessed
By bigger things than self and will can alter—

Only so much.

SCROLL TWO

Starvation was recommended,
But I thought a more radical approach might prove effective.
Death, in any form, had always interested me;

Even as a child I dreamed of landscapes
On the other side of sense and thought.
When the mountain viper bit me at nine and I survived,

My survival disappointed me; I was that eager
To get to the other side—but strange now, to be here, saying this:
I did not expect so much pain to linger,

I did not think so much pain could survive the flesh,
So much that seemed to hold me back outlive my bones;
Strange that so much of me still loiters here,

So much I tried to kill, still tarries unslain,
Undissolved by death, as yet unattuned
To this sudden absence of gravity, this exile from the senses.

Too much that has passed persists, awaited yet,
Somewhere in the flesh by some foetal form,
Some mortal womb, whose summons I am not permitted to refuse;

Too much endures: a pocketful of rattan seeds handed to me
By a dying uncle, which I had planned to string together
But never did; the touch of a hill-born girl

On a forested slope, and the edge of a railway bridge
Too often looked out from,
Where the tracks lead homewards, north,

Back to the low thatched huts and terraced rice fields,
The goat-studded slopes of a life no longer useful;
Or back, further north from home, to the unpeopled plateaus

And abandoned monastic strongholds of a decrepit culture,
Whose resurrection remains irreversibly postponed.
Too much persists: the hairless chest of a man I met in Mangalore,

With a dark blue lotus tattooed above his left nipple—
Beads from a broken rosary, and bright shreds of a robe
Worn by a monk who took each precept of his monkhood

More seriously than most and lost his way more often
Dazed by sermon-bred visions of absolute fullness,
Absolute nothingness, as he rummaged amidst ruins

For roots, imaginary moorings, the beguiling syllables
Between stupa and carven column, and the echoes of footfalls
In sculpted caves, of an incantation now unalterably defunct,

Reaching in, beyond the times of men, for the cave itself,
Groping for portals into prehistoric silences,
Or sealed in hotel bedrooms booked for the hour,

On streets that are home to more visceral hungers,
Set ablaze by army rum and powdered hemp—
Taut knots of nerves coming undone of their own accord,

In a joyous vortex of outflung limbs and loins,
An emptiness no different from the one envisioned,
Except that while it lasted it appeared to him

At once tangible and blissful, and that it left him wrecked—
His psyche parted between experience and belief,
His hands undone by loss of heat, quivering, delirious,

Till he returned, worsted by too many questions,
To that most exquisite chapter on the congruence
Of all consequence, the futility of all fruit,

The *Sammanaphala Suttanta*, with its irresistible tale
Of a liberated mendicant and an inquisitive elephant-mounted king,
His five hundred concubines trailing behind him,

Each with an elephant all to herself—
An image that had haunted me since boyhood.
Ah the soul has its own secret sculleries,

Its heaps of unwashed plates in forbidding basements
I was too scared in the flesh to walk down to,
And into which I am now summoned to descend.

Sing for me as I sink, pray for my passage,
Brothers whose trust I betrayed,
I who was blinded by angst, till I lost all sight of the hereafter,

And thought self-slaughter the nearest route to peace,
Or the surest way at least, to crawl up from the pit
Of being me. Men of my brotherhood,

Light up your lamps of oil, your incense sticks.

SCROLL THREE

The train I was to catch
Still leaves three times a week
From a station I could not make it to.

Swift frames of forbidding landscapes—brief village, grim township,
Inaccessible field, quickening desolation—
Cold scenes that deny habitation, sealed off by glass,

Slide past its passengers,
My brethren amongst them, orange-robed
And reassured by the belief

That they hasten towards some cherished centre,
Which each of them in turn was born to arrive at.
The train that lugs them on will have to break down perhaps,

Leaving them stranded, in some listless, inhospitable waste
Between two stations,
For them to see that they race,

Not further inwards from the periphery of life,
Towards envisioned redemption,
But helplessly around the centre they imagine.

The train they are on board will have to break down,
For them to see that when they arrive
At the place they are making for,

They will remain as removed from it,
As from those landscapes that pass them by
While the train still moves—

The train that takes them to Gaya,
Which I was to catch,
And which still leaves three times a week,

From a station I could not make it to.

SCROLL FOUR

Because being human is more than I have deserved,
And to exist is to want something, even in this dimension,
I request to be reborn amongst the higher mammals.

For to desire is to survive—
Though I know better now than to place my trust
In the prayer of the will; to believe

That some range of possible, assorted births
Might lie before one, simultaneously, for one's own choosing,
As shirts once seemed to hang in shopping arcades.

Though I am here to surrender the myth of choice,
Let the fleshless voice that I am wish on while it can—
No, not for the wings of mountain eagles, nor,

Though both have been considered,
For the serpent's infinite flexibility;
Only to be born amongst herds of wild elephants,

Deer or bison, amongst panthers or whales—
For this, because desire is survival, I pray:
Make me less than human but warm-blooded for sure,

Let gravity draw me, as a single maternal growl
From the throat of a mountain bear draws to her breasts
Her new-born cubs. Receive me, earth,

I lose sight of myself and feel your sudden weight.

Death at the Opera Comique

20 Rue de Gramont, 2ème Arrondissement, Paris, 17 July, 1990

i

The baroque caryatids would have been the last thing he saw—
Tall nonchalant women still content to bear the weight
Of a great florid building constructed for song,

His hunky avuncular arms flying swiftly past
A polished wooden nude from Haiti, a miniature from Ajmer
Poised against the open double-glazed windows

Of a terraced apartment that had served as servants' quarters
For Josephine Bonaparte. He would have walked
Up the steps to his wooden loft, past his immaculate

Self-carpentered tool cabinet, the whole room
With its acoustic flooring and the levered double bed
Upon which his fiancée lay asleep, self-designed—

A huge, hairy-chested beast of a man,
Athletic and in his prime, unable perhaps, suddenly,
To trust an interior of his own meticulous making—

Or seized by the horror of having to inhabit
The human heart, the impossibility of it,
Amidst the unreachable tranquillity of objects:

A six-stringed tanpura in a corner by the fireplace,
A Bavarian harp with a painted rose—
Amidst much we have no wish to think of,

That might have occurred,
In the presence of baguettes and a bottle of Bordeaux,
A seventh-century Sarnath Buddha, a slice of Camembert.

The police reported an accidental fall
At four a.m. outside the record store
In the basement of the Opera Comique.

We were told to believe what the police told us.

ii

My mother returned to Mumbai with a pair of his finest red
Rodolfo Valentino Italian leather shoes.
I felt fear the first time I stepped into them,

But wore them anyway, from one pubescent,
Beer-drenched party to the next.
I found the snakeskin buckles irresistible,

And came to feel, as I ran my fingers over them,
A longing to dance, a growing numbness
To the presence of death that compelled me to swirl.

I had fire in my feet back then—
Though now, in my forties, it makes me turn cold to think
I partied through my teens in a dead man's footwear,

Drinking myself stupid and dancing myself crazy,
Till I felt no fear of the dark that had seized him.
We recover in time lost reverence for the dead.

We forgive them their inability to look out of themselves,
As it grows harder to pretend we shall never be amongst them.
I see him dancing to the music of Zorba the Greek,

With all the brisk turns and startling jumps,
The intricate footwork all held in place,
As hard white plates whirl and crack about his feet,

Plummeting to smithereens against the mosaic floor
Of a Greek restaurant in the Latin Quarter—
A middle-aged, Parisian-Gujarati divorcee

Who spoke nine languages and worked as an engineer.
The dead must have their reasons to haunt us.
We begin to receive them as we would the living.

I like to leave him *here*, dancing.

Kamadeva Muses Upon the Death of the Body

Mahashivaratri, 2016

Who amongst the mountain-minded, the glacial seers,
The serpent-couched and lotus-seated;
Who amongst the all-fathering mentors,

The many-headed ones, wielders of strange weapons,
Or that great host of singers in celestial halls,
Commissioned forever to praise their presence—

Who amongst the great guardians of order,
The planetmasters, the lords of the eight directions,
Or the sages, kings and mortal prophets of earth,

Who amongst the gods can sing more truly than I,
The song flesh sings—or relate more clearly,
The tale of the soul's unyielding survival?

None more truly than I, Vasanta,
Primeval accomplice, dearest of seasons,
None surely amongst you, my siblings in the skies:

For I am Kamadeva, spirit of desire, survivor of fire,
Who has laughed and danced in the wake of the body's death;
O Kamadeva am I,

The fire in your loins that you may not fly;
No shape have I though the flesh is my home,
Your many arms my minions, your eyes my concubines,

As I quiver at the tip of your prurient tongues;
O Kamadeva am I—
Though the lord of the third eye

For his own hidden purposes
Assigns me to perpetual invisibility.
Be bold, season,

Confidante and companion ancient yet brief,
Bring out your blossoms, be the body I cannot be,
Wear all the colours I am not permitted to wear:

The warblers you summon, I teach them flight;
The hues you sport are my most fervent votaries,
And not a leaf, not a wing, not a limb, not a tail

Persists without my assistance. No, Vasanta,
Not a blossom can bloom where I choose not to be,
Which as you know, is almost nowhere,

Except where the master casts his third eye.
Ah, I shall not fear him, Vasanta,
Not tonight as on any other;

For night and I are ancient connivers,
And in the realms of the flesh I have nothing to lose.
Tonight, as on any other,

I shall crawl through the veins of beast and man,
Proclaiming triumph, or wrecking hearts doomed to wreckage—
O I shall sail upon churning oceans,

Cold seas of sweetened milk and hemp,
To witness the drowning of terrestrial lovers,
The success of my ploys in the courtyards of shrines;

And I will have the lovers of this world begging Shiva for mercy—
For I am Kamadeva, spirit of desire, survivor of fire,
O Kamadeva am I,

The fire in your veins that does not die;
The wise are deluded when they think I sleep,
For their loins are my vassals, their hands my cupbearers,

They who now gather, Vasanta,
These fervent multitudes furtively hearkening,
Hearkening to my cry, though none may ever see me,

For no shape have I, Vasanta: O Kamadeva am I.

Holika

Holi, 2016

i

Quintessence of all in woman best assigned to flame,
Demoness, witch, sorceress to most—
Yet martyr, saint and devotee to some,

I return with spring as in the year before,
To suffer amongst the living yet another immolation.
See: how soon amidst the songs and sudden blooms

Of this season, it grows into a cause for dance and merriment,
The re-enactment of my death.
Observe how relieved they appear

To be rid of me again, these pious throngs,
Now laved by the febrile ritual of my passing,
The annual firepurge before the morning's festivities.

I return for reasons rarely known to the living,
Best kept from them till they are ready to receive them;
For only the living can afford to question the ways of God,

And it is not for the dead to wonder,
Why we were chosen to play the parts we played,
No longer my part to question

This ecstatic survival of sons, this burning of women;
Or why my death each year,
Must remain for so many a cause for joy,

A great reason for song in the land I return to.

ii

Legend at times has attempted to be kind to me,
Suggesting I succumbed to the flames
Of my own free will, to keep the young prince from harm.

That is not what happened, of course;
I connived with the king for my own safety
And out of fear of pain—and it was God, as always,

God, interfering, irrefutable,
Who sent the gust that blew the shawl from my shoulders,
Throwing my body to the fire, protecting the boy.

I have no wish to be considered a saint;
Though there are those on earth who prefer
To believe my tale a tale of sacrifice.

There remains a place reserved for women like us
In the realms of the dead; a place for burnt women,
Who died so that the circle could be complete,

Hurt Nature healed, a great balance restored.
God, the human lion who clawed at my brother's guts,
Has in his mercy ensured

That our part in the tales of men,
Though invariably misremembered, may never be forgotten.
Now, as the heart of the north grows light,

Surrendering itself to colour;
And the insuppressible hues of hemp
Play out their games in the mind of man,

Recall our torched bones.
All you who still breathe, revering fire,
Who dance and drench yourselves

And lift your notes in jubilation at my death,
Keep at heart the black heap I was born to burn down to,
As you spray one another with brief jets of vermilion;

Revere the fire at the core of your dancing, your funeral pyre.

Mughal Sequence

(2012)

Mughal Sequence

I

HUMAYUN ATONES

One of his later 'miracles' or omens was when, after he had lost all his possessions and he was wandering in the desert, a solitary pack-camel appeared: it was laden with his most precious books...

—Rumer Godden, *Gulbadan*

They call me superstitious,
But this is only part of the truth:

Sure, there were times
When I foraged through your world for scraps of hope,

Scouring the stars and a thousand landscapes to learn,
If I would ever have my harem back, my gardens, my observatory—

But this was not what it was like
When I first looked at the zodiac signs embroidered on my tent,

Or years later, when I was drawn
To the upturned brows of a dying antelope,

A merchant in the desert,
With a single pomegranate left in his sack.

I wanted to know what these things were saying,
Not about me, my fortunes, or if and when

I would recapture the throne, but about themselves,

What they were saying about your world and how it moves.

Most of the time it was enough that you were speaking to me
Through all these images,

Regardless of what any of them might mean.

Opium I loved, as also your love:

Amongst the thousand voices of the poppy
I groped for your voice.

At times, I mistook my little blue tent,
With its painted stars, for your sky.

I sank through the quicksand that is behind the eye.

There was a man in green who said you had sent him,
A flamingo and a hawk,

There were turtles there, bigger than any I had seen,

A tambourine of poplars, white flakes of wind,

A veil of saffron that hid no face, brisk peals of laughter,

A lotus in the east that needed no lake to bloom in,

And upon the sand, an old scroll of odd phrases
Left to me by my father;

Phrases like clouds, placid horizontals,
That no longer cared to grow into lines.

I found no door to any life other than this,
Nor did I search feverishly.

Camels, cushions, the scent of turmeric, a jeweled inkpot,
And always at the edge of the desert, a cave full of ghosts:

A mellow brooding hung upon the air like fog.

I remember walking in—the tall grasses murmurous,
Sand on my tongue—but little thereafter.

I spoke with the dead but never as one of their company.

I lost all sense of weight. I burrowed. I writhed.

A taut muscular spiral held me in its grip,
Till I could see no sense in trying to move.

You hid. You came too close. You stayed for dinner, then left.

So much that had seemed to mean so much,
Shrank in that saffron haze.

When my lost camel appeared in the wastes of Sind,
I was half-asleep,

And it was those around me who took it for a sign
That I would be king once again.

Publicly, I agreed with them,
Because it seemed to keep them smiling;

But for myself, I was overjoyed
Simply to be back with my books.

All through that month I thought little

Of the kingdom I'd lost.
I spent a whole week postponing plans for war,

Rooting through my books for a line of verse
I could only half-remember.

For this and other obvious omissions, as a king,
And for being a hopelessly ungifted builder of empires,

I do not ask to be forgiven.

I made a better career as a reader of your world.

But for the blinding of my brother,
Who now begs, they tell me, in Mecca,

Your name on his lips,
Absolve me.

I was trying so hard to be an Emperor.

***

Falling is an idea
I have always been in love with.

Whenever I have been king,

I have been uncertain if I had nothing more
Than an empire, to defend or lose.

When I fell from the throne, I knew.

I learned slowly to befriend the pull of the earth;
Though still, I could only rarely bring myself

To rejoice in your ways.

I had a voice nobody else could hear
That summoned collapse,

A voice like a stream,
That could delight only in descent,

As it sang of loss,

And of the clarity that only comes
From losing oneself constantly.

And yes, I can see another fall coming,
Though I do not wish to consult the stars to know when.

It is enough to know that this time,
My fall from power shall be an act of praise.

There will be no fear then:

Only the stars, telling me nothing,
But singing amongst themselves,

Your name warm on my lips,
At home in my ears.

II

GULBADAN BEGUM IN SURAT, EN ROUTE TO MECCA

At Surat they were held waiting for a year, because their 'passes' were not in order; each pilgrim had to have a pass stamped with a picture of the Virgin Mary and the Infant Christ, because the Portuguese were masters of the sea. The ships were Turkish transports, with oarsmen for times when the wind dropped.
—Rumer Godden, Gulbadan

It was kind of the Emperor to come with me
All the way to Ajmer:

Dear old Akbar, reliable nephew,
King of kings,

Trying to please his aging aunt.
He came on foot at the head of the procession

Dressed in white;
And I am sure he honoured you in his heart as he walked;

Though he remains unable,
Being a man of power,

To recognize the singularity of your will,
The simplicity of your law.

I would make this journey on his behalf;

Yet know this is something I must do
For no-one but myself.

I ask you only to bless him as you have blessed me.

Visit him in his sleep. Warn him of his folly.

Ten months now,
And the Portuguese still show no signs of compliance.

They will use their images of Miriam
And the Prophet Jesus

To hinder anyone who longs to fulfil your will.

We have been here so long
That there are times now

When I catch myself preparing a speech,
A prayer for the day we arrive.

Silly of me, of course,
I know you're watching me rehearse.

Yes, I am eager to get on to that boat;
Though I know I have only to stop waiting,

To forget these distances.

The Tapi is adept at letting go of herself.

She knows there was nothing, in the first place,
To hold back.

So graceful a widening brings her to the sea,

That I have to remind myself she is not,
As the local infidels believe,

A goddess in her own right,
But simply a river, an aspect of your work.

My nephew the Emperor would probably agree with them.

He will have his bit
Of what he considers to be fun:

When we left Agra,
A loud celebration had just been held in his halls,

Commemorating the birth
Of a little blue thief who played the flute,

Born, the natives tell us, to save this world.

There was a frenzied clanging of cymbals,
A beating of drums, dancing,

And feverish recitals of demonic incantations
Praising this creature,

By a team of hired Brahmins,
Showered with pearls and gold.

He now plans to write to the Portuguese,
Asking them to send to his court,

A minister of their church,
To initiate him in their wayward doctrines,

And tutor his son.

I can see him kneel before a crucifix
And bow down before the brood of Satan,

His forehead smeared with vermilion and turmeric.

These are hard times, Lord, for the faithful:

A diabolical chanting resounds through our halls,
Where only silence and your word should be.

The works of the devil are now revered in our libraries,

The Quran placed on the same shelf
As books of lesser importance;

And the Emperor pays no heed
To the eye you cast upon him,

Your eye of wrath and terrible mercy;

Nor does he instruct his wives
In the wisdom of your ways.

Soon, they will hold a festival at the palace,

In praise of a bloodthirsty sorceress,
Whom they worship as divine—

But you know these things, of course,
I only say them because I need to.

What I fear most is not my death,
But the end of *our* world;

And your vengeance on somebody
Welded to me by love and blood.

Forgive him, Lord, his eagerness
To learn the ways of the infidel.

The Emperor is only a boy who wants to play.
Be merciful.

III

DANCING GIRL

To each Begum is to be delivered as follows: one special dancing-girl of the dancing-girls of Sultan Ibrahim, with one gold plate full of jewels—ruby and pearl, cornelian and diamond, emerald and turquoise, topaz and cat's-eye and two small mother-o'-pearl trays full of ashrafis.

—Babur, royal letter

I was born with a gift but now I have become one.

Kabul is cold.
Hardly the place to be dancing with naked feet.

The women I live amongst understand nothing
Of the craft I was bred for.

I would be lying if I said I no longer miss home,
Though I try not to dream of my years in the south.

The few friends I had died on our way here.

When those geese flew past the fortress turrets last night
I knew what I had guessed often before:

That all flight was impossible.

The stern ridges we crossed to get here,
Stare back at me now like the walls of a tomb.

They speak a tongue I am only beginning to learn.

When the Emperor's men came for us,
I knew our world had ended.

The commander-in-chief had me first,
Then the other soldiers who came to fetch me.

I gave myself with rehearsed compliance.
This ensured it would be over quickly.

I was neither broken nor enraged.
I am used to this sort of thing.

When we were taken from our homes
I pitied myself,

But feel sorrier now for the woman I serve—

Poor, closeted wretch,

Always so full of her busy, curtained self,
With never a glimpse of the simple way out.

Let her believe I beat this living earth with joy-stung feet,
Simply to please her;

That I endure this restive thrumming in the veins,
This dilemma in the muscles, this ache in the nerves,

I leap like a flame then fall like a hunted deer;

That I bind the deadly five before I befriend them,
Rejoice in the four,

I slice the fourteen into glittering smithereens of time,

I scatter, I glean, then swirl,

And make peace in a glance with the hostile north,
The hallowed east, the lost gardens of the south,

And the aging west;

That I twist and whirl, I careen and caper,

I admonish a meddlesome god,
Then stare him in the eye,

Only to enliven her listless afternoons.

Let her believe these lissome shoulders ripple,

These elbows lengthen into floating stems,

These fingers blossom into moonstruck lotuses,

At her command.

She has seen too little of either joy or servitude,
To guess what makes me move like this.

I dance because a demon commands me to—

Though I have known, at times, a steady swirling

That opened my ears to rumours in the blood
Of one greater than him I dance for—

But enough of this. I have been summoned.
There is this doorway and this arch,

A cold stone floor in an adjacent hall,
And no time now, for reflection.

There is this stubborn compulsion to move,
This ancient reticence in the muscles,

This fear, this lust and this primeval trembling
At the thought of the demon I serve.

A wreath of wild flowers to tie into my hair,
A cold wind from the mountains,

My string of brass bells,
The quivering of a drumskin,

The hall, the floor, the dance.

IV

BABUR, AFTER THE VICTORY AT KHANUA

But the vow he made before the battle of Khanua was different: this time the goblets and the cups were really broken up; some of the wine was poured into the ground, the rest had salt thrown into it to make vinegar and Babur kept his promise...but he still took what he called Majun, called in India, 'Bhang' and violently intoxicating.

—Rumer Godden, *Gulbadan*

Babur himself preferred to alcohol a drug which he calls majoon and he is very modern in his expression of its pleasures...but it is certainly an exaggeration to brand him, as he has been, an addict of either alcohol or drugs—apart from anything else his approach was far too orderly...

—Bamber Gascoigne, *The Great Mughals*

After some days of sorrow and repentance, we abandoned evil practices one by one, and the gates of retrogression became closed, but the renunciation of wine, the greatest and most indispensable of renunciations, remained under a veil in the chamber of deeds pledged to appear in due season, and did not show its countenance, until the glorious hour when we put on the garb of the holy warrior and encamped with the army of Islam against the Rajputs...An order was given that with the jihad, there should begin the still greater jihad which must be waged against sensuality.

—*Babur*, Royal Declaration Announcing the Renunciation of Wine 26 February, 1527 (translated by A.S. Beveridge)

Tonight I sing in praise of Majoon.

All through yesterday evening
The palace stank of ghosts.

When I ordered my men to fill the empty wine tank
With lemonade,

My little Gulbadan, my apple of joy,
Stared at me and laughed,

Then cupped her little hands, a minute later,
And drank.

I was ashamed of myself at once on two accounts:

For having been, for so long, such a drunken wretch,
And for being suddenly,

So much less of a man than I used to be.

Buff scraps of ripped wineskins glittered in the firelight,

My finest carpets smeared
With fragments of smashed goblets,

Magenta and russet, lavender and maroon:

Shards of a chalice,
The sharp handle of a jug,

And all night the hideous, indelible sound
Of the breaking of pots and the cracking of clay cups

Echoing through the palace courtyard,
Like the tuneless squawking of a great trapped swan,

Cheated, by murderous hands,
Of its right to a final song.

This sound,

And that merciless gushing and spilling,
That diligent casting out of wine,

Set loose in my halls a hot host of fiends with wings of flame;

Bright spirits of ire, forcibly unhoused,
Enraged at our assault upon their ancient homes

In the bellies of decanters, the slim necks of old phials.

Some flew to the ceiling and lodged themselves in cornices,
Some followed me to my chamber,

Some hid behind cushions,
Or fled like crows at the throwing of a stone—

But one of them, bolder and more subtle than the rest,
Wore my face as a mask,

And loomed before my bed and gripped me with his eye,

Then crept, at my own depraved, tormented pleading,
Beneath my quilts,

And held me tight in the vice of his long arms and thighs,

Seizing my trembling tongue with his,
Till all speech dissolved into the taste of his mouth.

I struggled like a girl,

Pushing against the great stone wall of his chest
As he crushed and ravished me,

Meeting the weight of his body with strength,
Till I knew his fire to be greater than mine,

And stopped fighting.

For what seemed like a lifetime,
We stayed like this together: awake, without moving,

Thick petals of florid sandstone quivering in the morning breeze,

Till the hand of the All-merciful wafted me to brief sleep,
Then cast me once again upon the shores of the living.

I rode out into the field sober at dawn.

I feared neither death nor defeat;
Only the absurdity of meeting the enemy drunk.

Now thanks unto Allah for my victory at noon,
And praise unto Allah for last night's defeat.

Taut images of heat still haunt my halls,
Scorched remains of a night only half outlived.

I reach out, with singed fingers, for my daughter's hand,

And wine still scours the burnt forests of the heart
Like a bruised tigress summoning a lost cub.

But praise be unto Allah for I am cured;
The thought of all that fire no longer allures me.

I turn it over in a breath to the guardian of my heart,

And sense in my veins the first uncertain gusts
Of a mountain wind fresh from Kabul,

City of spice and samite, fine sugar and slaves.

No hillside spring in blessed Ferghana—
Valley of stout pheasants, abundant grain and fruit—

Could ever be clearer than I now am.

I rejoice in the private movements of things
That pretend to be still:

In the deft manoeuvres of flowerpots and knives.

Or the shifting gaze of a lacquered screen,
Where a birdcage awaits me and mirrors stand sentinel.

Let my soldiers gulp their feverish dregs like swine.
Let them laugh their febrile, obsidian-eyed laughter,

And swamp themselves with tears of fire,
Then glare at each other

With that old angry itch in their eyes,
Like peasant boys looking for a fight.

I sense a music more verdurous,
A less cumbersome grief, a more graceful pang,

A laughter that is much lighter than theirs,
And rejoice to sit apart from their company,

In the fellowship of Majoon and the smell of lemonade;

For I am enamoured of ice tonight,

And understand clearly now, the words of the Prophet
Concerning wine,

Though his need to be a king puzzles me,
As does my own.

Wine I acknowledge as the workmanship of Satan,
Majoon, the Maker's gift to malaised mankind.

This evening, before sundown,
The Colour Green visited me, and stayed with me through supper,

Till I knew myself to be no host,
But a guest in his halls.

Babur, tiger, emperor,

You who have belonged for so long
To a family of movable things

That you begin now to comprehend their furtive ways,

The life of a jewelled inkpot, a carpet, a collapsible desk,
A cushion, a dagger, an embroidered tent;

Babur, tiger, emperor,
Victor, father, commander and spouse,

Pride of the Chagatai, Mongol, Turk,
Descendant of lame, indomitable Timur, untamable Genghis,

And a virgin ravished by a stray, concupiscent moonbeam;

Pillager of villages, planter of orchards,
Grower of bananas and sugarcane, and sower of a terrible seed;

Mountain-gazer, tunic-mender,
Seal-engraver, falcon-trainer, saddle-binder, bandit;

Truant of the Oxus, Satyr, nymph, and tramp of Transoxiana,

Rhymester, gamester,
Lover of wild tulips, fountains and boys;

Chronic nostalgist, inveterate melancholiac,

Pariah, vagabond, winesoak, lech,
And relentless compounder of unyielding antonyms;

Babur, tiger, emperor,

Builder of princedoms and treacherous ramparts,
Architect of couplets, sculptor of epithets,

Mason of quatrains and finite lists,
And breaker of hearts and temples, idols and oaths,

Farewell.

May the tombs of my heirs outsoar my own;
For Majoon now strips me of these histories I wear,

And I hear the low droning of a string in a rosary of notes;

An ancient, mind-defeating music surfacing afresh
Amongst the people of these plains,

Its quartertones riddled with the silences of the Sufis,

Its cadences kindled by the flames of Zarathushtra,
And gentle as the breathing of Jesus,

Its rhythms spawned in the fervent veins of the infidel;

A music weaned upon the milk of Persia,
Bred by the Indus, and guarded

By the wakeful mountains of the North.

I hear strong freezings,
A hailstorm of hardened notes, sharp icicles of sound,

Then the thrumming of the blood,
Where a man and his fate clang against each other

Like a pair of cymbals in the hands of a local priest:

The moaning of the marrow in its womb of bone,
And songs composed for the weddings of winds,

The mating of the musics of hill and plain,
While quilts of wind swaddle me asleep

And blithe beams of healing sapphire lull me awake;

A cold, benevolent light
That unmakes me gently to its own strange ends,

And whose ways I remain, as always, a slave to,

As it puts to rest a conqueror's schemes,
And knocks at the soul of a hill-spawned child;

Light that urges the beast to walk out into the night
And teaches the scholar to blow out his candle.

I make way for these signs as these plains have made way
For those who were bred here,

And rejoice to know that these hills watch over me,
That this river is my sister, this body my tent.

In the libraries of Majoon be this minute preserved,

For I listen once again with the ears of a rock,
To the sound of water falling.

I see a torrent of ghosts, a multitude of horses,
And Thought's generals unhorsed as my harness comes loose.

I see this and make room,
Amongst the hard-clutched shards of a lying history,

And carcass heaps of abandoned selves,
For the perilous minute of untainted habitation:

Territories of the breath unvisited by nostalgia,
Wide, shadowless and asking not to be ruled,

Only lived in.

I see empires of form dissolving like salt,
Collisions of planets, the violence of beasts,

And viridescent oceans churning at noon,
As Time's citadel yields to green armies of joy,

His bastions battered, his markets overthrown,
Troupes of lissome spirits careening jubilant

Through vanishing streets.

I see this and see also,
As in the shadow of a rainless cloud,

The bright cobalt dome of Timur's tomb in Samarkand,

A taciturn mural,

A narrow, soul-sheltering frieze in a joyless pavilion,
Glimpsed at in a hurry,

Through the nervous eyes of a dying adolescence;

A portico etched with leaves,
A low blue alcove composed of stars,

Strong pillars of silk, a mosaic that refused me,
White pediments of petals ruffled by no breeze—

Then an open square with a quadrant at its heart,
That refuses to make plain what it knows about the sky,

Clinging, like a jealous father,

To the rightful spouse of a primordial riddle,
Hoarding true knowledge,

Screening the death of paradox with its veils of stone:

Curtains of basalt, alleyways of musk,

And the nine gardens of the city,

Gardens coveted and possessed, entered and lost;
City of bewitchment, jubilation and failure;

Of the turquoise gateway
That unfastened its bolts to summon me home;

And whose pointed arch I fled,
Hoping to inhabit my loss with grace.

I see the lips of the Shah of Persia, smiling,
As he sips his wine from his neighbour's skull;

And a square brick tower decked with the heads of defeated kings,
An empty niche on its westward face,

Intended, for my own.

May Allah acquaint me with my love of defeat,

May Allah bring me where defeat
Wakes from her dreams to her morning feast,

Droning, in her voice like a lake,
Her first low note in praise of earth.

May he build me a home where loss grows beautiful;

And may Allah always help me recall
The voice of a eunuch in my father's harem

Singing me to sleep with a verse from the Quran.

I see the sand that rises from the hooves of a thousand horses,
Settling at noon by the caravanserai,

An ibex amongst the narcissi on a hillside path,

And maternal palms driving me to my bridal tent,
When all I wanted was a cup of wine.

Wingbeats of pigeons, a stool of gold and mother-of-pearl,

And the single feather I found of a large brown pheasant
I could never hunt down.

A dovecote on a fortress tower,
A woven screen,

A talisman with a bearclaw, a necklace of coins,
The brasswork on the hilt of my father's sword,

The minarets at Herat, the breasts of a slave,
The smell of rice and vegetable stew.

I see the faces of glaciers gathered like crones:

Twilight on the Oxus,
Kababs on hot coals, scent of roast venison,

The anxious braying of a three-legged mule,
The strumming of a ribab—

And I remember marvelling

At how indifferently night came down
On either side of the river—

Then hoofbeats in the valley, the quivering of bowstrings,
Great drums and horns,

And large flocks of geese taking flight
At a shrill clanging of scimitars:

Blood on my sleeves, vultures, carnage, crows
And rich fields of wheat, sesame and mustard, burning, burning;

Thatched roofs on fire, the deep bellow of a cannon,
A herd of deer in a field of poppies;

A bridge of rope across a hillside brook
Sporting its sudden wings of flame,

And quiet, in the hallowed shade of a hunchbacked ridge,
Crowned by the slenderest of crescent moons,

The ragged tent of a mendicant sufi.

I felt fear the first time I entered that tent—

I, who walked in with the mind of a hawk
Perched on a wrist it could not see,

Conjuring a world beyond its hood—

I watch the lakes of this world outsurge their margins,
Stone bridges collapse,

And the peaks of the Hindukush drown in their streams.

I see a people forever at war with History
And obsessed with language,

A sea of smouldering millet, oceans of torched wheat,
The charred remains of a village I had loved,

Burnt to the ground at my command.

I see a dark mound of headless torsos
Bundled into knots by the edge of a well,

And heaps of lopped arms still looking for home.

I feel the panting of a girl, the grief of mothers.

I see battalions of belligerent shepherds,
And herds of soldiers with wings like swans.

Cracks in a high mud wall, featherscent,
The voice of a wild fowl echoing in a cataract;

The cold frets of an unstrummed oudh in a gardened courtyard,
A rivulet in a cleft;

Wars, meadows, murders, weddings, plunder, music,
Saddles, cradles, lances, lakes;

A pair of cranes in a field of sunflowers; and faces, faces:

The guileless eyes of a nomadic herder,
Staring for the first time, at a matchlock aimed at his flocks;

The taut, moonscorched face of a lovelorn cousin scaling the walls
Of bewitching Samarkand;

The frozen gaze of a severed head
I carried off as a trophy at fourteen;

And etched into this sky, soaring immaculate
Above this welter of terrestrial forms,

Quiet and distant as a paper kite
Whose sharp string my grazed, untutored fingers

Let slip forever,

The face of a boy
Who is still searching for me,

Amongst the market-tents of Kabul;

Whose body I borrow from time—
His lips the nascent lines of an unutterable couplet—

Then yield, like a child, to his Maker's will;

For I hear an aging voice upon the air,

That cautions me against too much looking
At this advancing phalanx of summoned images I cannot command,

His face its apex,

Their burnished spearheads raised and aimed
At what remains of the beast in me to kill.

Allah, be merciful, inform me of my defeat—

But peace:

Let there be less talk of such things,
For tonight I sing in praise of Majoon,

In Turki and Arabic, Hindustani and Persian;

I learn to watch without taking sides—

Having won upon the field,
What remains, in mortal terms, a victory—

This war in my head, and in heaven and on earth,
Between the angels of joy and the angels of meaning.

Praise be unto the Omnipotent,

And to his living messenger on earth,
His most potent and loving servant,

The benign, compassionate, all-mothering Angel of Majoon.

Out, my soldiers, with your trumpets, your lutes and carven horns,
Pound your low drums,

And lift in praise of the spirit who moves amongst us,
A frenetic shout—

But no, mute your rough voices, abjure your instruments,
And glut your souls upon the devil's strong wine;

For they alone who have risen from the ranks of the grape
And lain with the Angel,

Who have slept in the furnace and woken in the snow;

And dared to watch their dwellings burn
That they may touch the ice of glaciers;

They alone who have sickened with age of their own anxious breathing,

And seeking no lordship over sultanates of heat,
Live on to learn that this world is home;

Who outlive the familiar lure of disaster,
The longed-for pang, the delirium of rage,

And are lifted from the terrors of the devil's warm brew;

They alone who have tunnelled through the netherworld of wine,
Abandoned its bleak, cerebral labyrinths,

And emerged from its chasms, embracing air,
Standing at guard, eye-to-eye with frenzy,

Alert in a glance to the ancient mistake,
And torn from their haggard masks of wrath;

Who have learnt to welcome dusk,
Looking out, beyond the ruins they have become,

Where darkness grows habitable;

Who know the joy of being small,
And no longer build their prisons of tears,

Their turrets of hubris and citadels of fear;
They who have let their hearts' enduring battlements

Be battered and beaten and broken by their brains,
Till their brains deserted them and the Angel received them;

They alone amongst men must aspire to such praise.

Back, my men, to your jars and flagons;

For I will not have you praise, at my command,
What you know so little of,

And *I* must be led where none can follow.

In the history of praise be this breath remembered,
In the mansions of Majoon may this song resound;

And leave room, my angel, in my praising, for lament,
For no praise comes easy,

And all must be unlearnt at the turn of each breath.

I hear the wordless tones of the last couplet
In the throat of the Angel of Majoon upon the Day of Judgement,

Its lines a pair of eagle's wings,
Gliding to a halt, as if to say: 'hush'.

I hear this,
And between two breaths I am content,

Yet reach through a haze of tone for words,
Hoping to mimic its receding tread;

Or obscure, perhaps, what I dare not hear.

For the span of a wingflap,
The semblance of a syllable, the first bones of a clause:

Then nothing, no-one. Then no-one but me,
Wronged by no other and wrecked by pure sound,

Befuddled by absence, invaded by History,
And hunted by a syllable that refuses to be born,

My arms upraised, my seasons confused,
My ears at war with the musics of this earth,

As I stumble through speech,
With a line on my lips that has clung to them for decades;

That rejects the varied grooms I diligently bring her,
And awaits in silence her predestined beloved.

It may be that my couplet will never form,
Or be too simple, when it does, to remain poetry.

But be this as it may,

I throw out my nets against the wind,
When my heart's like the Oxus in flood,

Listening for the gap between croon and cry,
As I leap upstream for its rhythms like a mountain trout,

Then grope through clouds for the turn of a line,
Seeking, like an inconsolable ghost,

To wring from the noondry debris of an outlived life,
Young tones of praise.

Deliver me from History, Angel, unsaddle my veins.

For here, within the courtyard of this chest,
The inner precincts of these loins,

Is the body I have always longed to walk into:

Twelve tongues now congregate at the tip of my tongue,
To lift the weight of my artless shout.

Here, in my mouth, they gather and wait, breathing deep
Till they take my leave,

And scour my halls for less peaceful men.

Release me from History, Angel, untutor my lips;

And over those realms that visit me in sleep,
May I never seek dominion.

I hear the murmurous beginnings
Of a nascent phrase upon the lips of sleep:

Rumours of blue tiles, orange trees and musk,
And verdant syncopations of pheasant cries and lutes.

My veins grow wings,

And night makes herself at home in sudden clearings
Urging me on where no image may walk.

I embrace the dark and praise the light.
I sing in praise of Majoon tonight.

V

THE KOH-I-NOOR

It was finally forwarded to Queen Victoria, arriving in time to become the prize exhibit in the Great Exhibition of 1851.
—Bamber Gascoigne, The Great Mughals

Here, in this tower,
Bound by gold clamps to thin walls of gold,

I, who am pure mineral, neither mortal nor ghost,
Remain doomed to abide.

Of those who are sent here only the living escape.

I endure the doom of rock,
Inhabited by light and never at home—

No, never, never for a minute
Since I was taken from the stomach of this earth,

Except, perhaps, through the week I dreamed unguarded,
Unpraised and unpossessed,

In the waistcoat pocket of a British lieutenant
Who thought me worthless.

Most men who held me beheld only what I showed them,
And I saw much that their pride could not begin to see,

Though monarch and vassal alike,
Minion and minister, eunuch and page,

Cupbearer, concubine, courtesan and queen,
Only rarely guessed that I was watching.

I have seen too many blindings,

Too many tremblings of oil lamps
In mirrored paternal halls usurped by the young:

The banishment of music,
And the nervous weaving of recalcitrant cotton,

Where fountains had leaped and the peacock once danced;

Too many orgies, too much opium, and too much penitence,

Too many depraved flailings in the courtyards of mosques,

And self-assured mastectomies of prurient goddesses,
By incensed, believing hands,

To be moved or repulsed, intrigued or deceived.

These things I have seen, and seen myself too often now,
In the sculpted faces of mute attendants,

While ailing emperors clung to me in their slumber,

Then woke before death,
Envious of my transparence, but unaware of my gaze,

Staring right through me with opiate eyes
Or eyes vermilion with wine.

I, who have never cared to be a seer,
Have seen these things,

And ask only now,
To be sheltered from the light that can never be mine.

Return me to the mines.
Carry me back to the dark that scorned me.

From *Elephant Bathing*

(2012)

Bitter Gourd

Sixteen years now, and I have looked too often
Into certain mirrors, searching for self-love,
Yet hoping to find, reflected there,
Your eyes, looking over my shoulder.

And now that you are here finally,
I see you, not by reflection, but eye to eye,
Looking back through your eyes across half my life,
Wondering what else you could have done back then,
But teach me slowly to hate myself;
You, who showed me so early in life,
How the seeds of bitterness are best sown in silence,
Best swallowed alone.

Here, have some bitter gourd slices.
They are all I have cooked this morning,
As fate would have it,
Half-knowing, as always, that you would come;
And I have made them thin, the way you liked them,
Dry, brown, and crisp to the seed,
Stir-fried, with just enough salt,
Over a slow fire.

Nineteen Forty-two

August wounds him. His friends play games in which he does not join.
His mother is a woman who lives in a cage.
She is there for the Nation, his father tells him.
That man in brown with the big black keys must *be* the Nation,
He concludes, and aims a pebble at the jailor's groin.

The boy who casts this innocent stone is only seven;
But soon he will befriend the frets of an old sitar,
Urging the strings to embrace desertion,
Conjuring a lost void, till they are taut with images
He cannot bring himself to remember; or cry to be forgiven

For crimes he did not commit yet fears his own. The Mahatma
He will come to view, with an awkward, half-tormented
Reverence; and of course, he will be drunk often, proclaiming
In his drunkenness that Gandhi was a great man, though his followers
Were mostly fools—prisoners of a barren blinkered dogma

That numbed them to colour and made them believe the sacred flesh dirty.
The use of Gujarati he will forbid amongst his sons—
A coarse unmusical purely functional tongue
That Gandhi thought in, for Gandhi, though of course a great man,
Was wholly unmusical—and then, on an evening, approaching fifty,

He will call home for drinks his raucous bunch of ageing whiskey-swilling
Peers; and they will talk of simpler days, when the streets were clearer,
Houses bigger, and the world more habitable, quaffing them down,
Till he produces out of his pocket, as a sort of joke, a miniature Union Jack
And a quizzically brown, fading photograph of a dead British king,

Crooning to himself, till everyone joins in, that surging drone of a song,
That invokes an alien biblical god—
And which they all remember standing up for
On schoolboy visits to the cinema, when films were only black and white—
Its cadences turgid, frozen almost, as the long

Last note billows out of the living room like a windy tent,
And they drain their glasses in quick nostalgic gulps—
All this, at two in the morning, while at the other end
Of the same long-corridored house, his mother, insomniac,
Knits little dolls for orphaned girls; or looks up from nascent

Amorphous snippets of Gujarati verse at a moonless street,
Her husband awake beside her, up for her sake; both of them
Too tone-deaf to recognize, or be briefly wounded
By the drunken anthem their son lifts in praise
Of an empire they waited so long to defeat.

August 15, 2006

Tidal Wave

Believe me,
I didn't mean to do this.
I believed, with the seers and ecstatics,
That the sea would bring me
Where I needed to arrive,
That no amount of lunging shorewards or holding back,
Could alter anything about to happen.
I began as a tremor,
A shudder in the brooding loins of the sea,
That set me moving to no visible end.
Her sway seemed to hold all motion in place
And I dreamed of nothing that breathed beyond her skin,
Was granted no visions, as she urged me on—
Spurring me out of her, yet tightening her grip—
Of the fields I would swamp, the children I would drown,
The homes I would crush with soft claws of water.
Nor could I tell,
As those doomed coasts drew near,
That in their ruin lay also my own;
Or the end, at least,
Of the only chance I thought I had
Of being truly born,
Of being anything more than an aspect of sea.
Unspawned, I remain now as ghosts remain,
A voice in the veins of those who survived me
That clings to a theme they long to forget—
Yet hear me now,
Women of the coast, offspring of the dead,
You whose progeny I snatched from your arms,

Whose crops I wrecked and whose cattle I killed,
Hear me and see how softly I speak:
No roar. No crash.
No surging crescendo, no deafening cascade,
No rapt interjections of spindrift and surf;
And no more of that turgid, moon-depraved magniloquence
That brought me briefly to believe myself
A being apart from the sea that bore me.
Friends of the departed, lovers of the drowned,
Hear me when I say I had no will in this matter.

Elephant Bathing

He will never go there again,
Hip-flask in pocket, camera at hand,
Far from the crowded confines
Of the human animal he could not trust,
To the lush cricket-choired thickets
He so jealously loved;
Dense, creeper-canopied spaces
Where he would listen eagerly
For the sudden slither of a python's tail,
Or the persistent mating calls of leopard and crane,
Studying the stealthy ways of predator and prey,
Till panther, bison, hyena and stag
Seemed part of a single guileless continuum
He had only begun to see his part in.
Now home and city hunt him down,
Building about him their busy labyrinth
Of doctors, nurses, brothers and sons;
Though tiger and spotted deer remain,
Frozen above his bed in black and white.
An egret pecks noiselessly at a crocodile's jaws,
As pale flamingoes, stripped irretrievably of their pinks,
Leap into a flight forever deferred.
Where you are going, they seem to say,
You will have no need for us or all you remember.
And yet the thought of getting there is not unlike
A great lone tusker taking the plunge,
His vast grey bulk sinking below the riverline

Against a clear black sky,
Till there is no more of him to see
Than a single tusk,
White as a quarter-moon in mid-July,
Before the coming of a cloud.

Dead, at Your Mother's Funeral

As if to quench the first, flickering wisps of flame,
Rain poured in torrents when I reached the grounds,
Beating wildly upon the low tin roof,
Like a great hurt beast no will could tame.

Sweat covered your forehead, your blue sleeves wet,
As you took the hot brand into your palms,
Turning towards me before you lit the sticks,
Your brown hair drenched as when we first met.

Can I say I still loved the man I saw,
Whose loss I turned so quickly away from?
I saw you through tongues of leaping flame,
And cold eyes of ice no flame could thaw,

Your mother burning as I thought of my own,
Seeking no way into the cell of your grief;
No way out of mine as I heaped her with twigs,
Poured oil on damp wood and watched you like a stone.

My Father's Old Man

Summer that year had come to an early close.
Rain beguiled us with its cryptic promise of renewal
And the jackfruit tree still clung to its ripened fruit,
When he gave me his watch and his bunch of keys,
And his dead wife's file of verse and prose.

For the first slow fortnight after she died, he was too worn-out
Even to bathe; but then he took to watching television,
And studying the morning paper when he could.
At first we took turns, my father and I,
Helping him with his list of things to be bought

To keep the house running, wading through absence,
Looking out beyond hope for the oarless raft of his grief.
We wreathed her photograph with lilies and marigold,
And talked of cricket, politics and the state of the stock market,
Hoping that our chatter would drown out her silence.

But as the months drew on, we drew back in fear
From those mordant, phantasm-peopled spaces
That homed in on his pain; and once a week, when he shaved,
We feared the bitter conundrums his tilted mirror posed:
That voice thrumming at the back of his head—was it him or her?

Was the flesh his guest or his ailing host?
We had no answers and dared not guess, or seek
To tune our deadened nerves to the pitch of his loss,
Till a month before the end, we left him alone,
With a hired night nurse and his wife's mute ghost,

An old wooden bed and a God to thank,
And locked ourselves in separate adjacent rooms,
Our whiskey consanguineous, a febrile sealing
Of troubled veins and bonds, and a sealing-off:
We let the man die while we dreamed and drank.

Tusker Kills Mahout at Religious Festival

An elephant runs riot while carrying the body of the mahout it killed at the Chettuva Chandanakkudam Festival in Vadanapalli, Thrissur district, Kerala. At least seventeen people were injured during the incident.
—Photo caption, *Times of India*, 13 April, 2007

Nine weeks now, and the tamarind tree has put out a new branch.
A fresh wind from the west, the first rains.

The men barely notice me now on their way to the fields.

The womenfolk walk past me nonchalantly
On their way to the river.

The village pundit is punctual about his weekly exorcisms:
Rosewater. Turmeric. Sandalwood. Ash.

Only the children still fear me.

***

A local poet has composed a paean
In praise of what he sees as my rebellion,

My willingness to be ruled by nothing
But an ancient impulse to break free.

The nation, he sings, has much to learn from this.

The villagers who hear him are amazed
That a demon so vile

Should have dared to lodge itself in *me*,
A beast half-divine, the mortal god of their tribe.

They tell him the same demon now lives in his songs.

***

Sure, they have their reasons, all of them,
Poet and pundit, men and women of the village,

For believing what they believe;
But all it was, really, was lust,

A minute's raw lust for a dead mate,
That tore me from my senses:

A huge haze came over me. A chaos
Of people and rocks, clouds, fields, hills and trees,

A compelling smell that meant: *her skin.*
Gravity deserted me, my light legs floated,

My body convulsed,
Then threw itself back before I knew it.

I trampled fences, crushed a thatched hut.
I uprooted a mango sapling not yet three summers tall.

When I lifted his broken body into my trunk,
I was not sure if he had hit the ground,

I was that uncertain about where the earth really was.

Nobody understands that I was trying to save him.

***

My new mahout is a good man.

He brings me fruit and wreaths of flowers at dawn
And says his prayers before he mounts me:

A wishful man, incorrigibly credulous,
Who trusts his gods and believes my demon has left me for good.

I have no wish to hurt him,
I do not resent the guiding strokes of his iron goad.

But I have only to think of her again, in that way,
And I am sure I will kill him.

Ghazal

after Agha Shahid Ali

Shall I hold my tongue, lord, or call tonight?
Contain myself, or start another brawl tonight?

My dead mentor returns. Shall I silence him with words,
Or wrap his image in a shawl tonight?

I am lured by the dark I longed to outgrow.
I long to crawl back into that caul tonight;

And the words of the saints fade like bad dreams.
Their voices will not fill this hall tonight.

Leave me, Lord, leave me alone with my song,
For I shall not be your thrall tonight;

And leave the door open, behind you, when you leave.
I have another guest to enthrall tonight:

Come, my heart, let us be friends again,
And celebrate the ancient fall tonight.

Negotiating Negativity on the Western Ghats

I have waited all morning for this fog to clear,
Looking through its folds for stray signs of green;
Yet now that the terraced slopes and paddy-fields
And the woods that it hid draw steadily near—

The thick moss on a branch, the full height
Of a hill, and the lily-spotted weir
Shimmering insistently in late noon heat—
The eye retreats in fear from approaching light;

And I long more strongly for the fog to come down,
Covering in a single length of shroud
The bright greens it wrapped in torn scraps of grey,
And the watcher outside whom it would not drown.

Vast spirit of presence, untutor my eyes.
Cast them into this swirl of grey and green,
Till they come to feel at home in change.
Grant them the craft of swift goodbyes.

Glacier

One might have been born for such sharp alignment:
The white curve of an arch quietly concentric

To the bowl of my skull, my knees midway
Between a pair of columns, the feet of a chair

In line with my palms, as walls and bookshelves,
Window, ceiling, lampshade and guitar

Converge silently round the axis of my spine.
Now couched on straw matting and niched in wide spaces,

The body might even be a hub of strong forces,
A pivot or a nucleus but for which

These walls might give way, these rafters cave in.
The stone Buddha on the shelf no longer

Asks me to probe myself; nor does the jug on the table
Urge the eye, to forage for any meaning

Beneath its jet black. The smooth curves
Of its sides would have me stay as I am,

Wide-eyed and becalmed by the surfaces of things
Willfully arranged to centre me;

And it might be wise, if I could, to stay true to their will;
But I have only to shut my eyes to know at once

That I am a vast frozen mountain thawing in the sun,
Huge, heaving chunks of me breaking off at random,

Crashing with a thud into the river below;
The strong, single-minded river,

That is always letting go of itself,
That may possess no single centre of gravity,

And knows no direction but downhill and seawards.

Vacillations of a Recondite Nudist

> *Take no thought from morning unto evening and evening*
> *unto morning for what ye shall put on.*
> —St Thomas

Swaddled in white quilts and buttoned up tight—
No lover asks me why this must be so—
I will not sleep in the nude tonight.

They outleap themselves who leap into sight.
Can the arrow but fear the tightening bow?
Swaddled in white quilts and buttoned up tight.

Bright mirrors urge me to stay away from light.
What if there is no-one here to know?
I will not sleep in the nude tonight.

Do the naked ascend undaunted by height?
Is it only by casting off we grow?
Swaddled in white quilts and buttoned up tight.

Must the string be left to the will of the kite?
The question appeals but the answer is no,
I will not sleep in the nude tonight,

Though swans wear nothing when they break into flight—
For who can endure the slow letting go?—
Swaddled in white quilts and buttoned up tight.
I will not sleep in the nude tonight.

Living Room

I understand that you do not wish to change.
Your walls have grown so used to silence,
To staying bare and tough; and they must find it strange
To be coaxed into this new exuberance—

But you have housed the dying for long enough,
Their ghosts freer now, to visit you at their will,
Than when they needed you, in the flesh,
To keep chaos beyond the edge of the sill.

And will your arches still curve so reclusively,
As if to hold on to the half-dark of tinted glass?
Now brighten your fruit bowl with oranges,
Roll up your blinds and burnish your brass,

Fill your armchairs with guests, your decanters with gin,
Unhinge your doors and let the world in.

Steam Bath

I cannot tell if he is someone I know:
The naked man in the corner, whose face this steam obscures,
Colluding with crushed hemp and an ancient ache,
And unfurling its billows to form, as it froths and pours,

The face of a man whose angst I have touched,
Whose lust I have clutched and harboured like a clone;
His bleak misgivings now nearly mine,
His lips of steam closing in on my own,

To claim their insistent predatory kiss.
I am wise to his way of assuming congruence.
I smile at the furrow in his narrowing brows.
He cannot become me when I breathe like this—

But will I leave here, undaunted by his fears,
Redeemed by heat when I reach for this door;
Or will he follow me softly across this floor:
The man I have longed to sweat out for years.

Duet on the Death of a Cat

Two monks were fighting over a cat. The master appeared, drew his long sword, and sliced the cat into two halves. 'Here,' he said, 'is your cat, and here is yours.' The words of the koan must not be interpreted, only received.
    —Ritesh Reddy, second-degree black belt, private lecture.

We've left here before but this time we're through.
The master's a hustler, a monster, a fake;
And he's sliced our pretty little cat in two.

Surrender's our motto, but this simply won't do.
Have we nothing but a pair of selves at stake?
We've been here before but this time we're through.

Who rends this mesh, ends this myth of me and you?
The long tail reaches back for the mouth of its snake;
And the master has sliced our cat in two.

No sign to decipher. No vision. No clue:
If death is not real, whom does death unmake?
We've been through this before but this time we're through.

Someone could tell us what this means, but who?
Who puts us to sleep, who shakes us awake?
The master has sliced our cat in two.

Time for this ship to abandon its crew—
But we're *thinking* again, the ancient mistake—
We've left here before but this time we're through.
The master has sliced our cat in two.

The Buddha Above the Window

How soundlessly they gather around him now:
Those shed contorted shapes

Whose lives he had thought it his lot to lead.
Deft imposters that had him believe

They were his reason for walking this earth;
Beguiling robes,

That clung to his skin like his own dark hair,
Binding his nerves in thick knots of thought,

Yet asking nothing of him, in essence,
Except to be worn:

Father, lover, seeker, prince,
Their anxious tones no longer clutter

The rimless gap of his watchful repose.
Yet around the wood that frames this form,

This wishful hub of muted orange,
Bestowed by playful, dying hands

On one whom forms no more confine,
A troubled music broods and brews

That concerns itself relentlessly with paradox,
Its turgid arrivals and cryptic surgings

Incorrigibly at odds with the drone that spawned them,
An impassioned negation disguised as praise

For some imagined primordial pulse
That they claim descent from or seek to return to;

Each restive pause,
A veiled refusal to be inhabited by space;

An adept yet all-too-eager attempt at emptiness,
Turbid with nostalgia for known destinations,

As it reaches out of itself and beyond the sill,
For a realm already present within these walls;

A realm of things already in place
That remain unmoved by its taut manoeuvres

And lend no ear to its trenchant urgings:
Bottles, bookshelves, cupboards, mats,

Creepers, clouds, moonlight, rugs,
A porcelain vase, a candlestand, an antique clock,

A neighbour's yellow sarong put out to dry,
And the ficus poised in silence

Against night's familiar absences:
A wilting stem, the putting out of a leaf.

Housewarming

I was conceived in a tent:
The savannahs talkative, brief rain after dusk,
The risen moon a slim crescent above cratered Kilimanjaro.

And amongst those humming tides of grass
Vibrant with the memory of wildebeest hooves,
Those campfires, mudpaths, jeeptracks, ropes,

And cloudless shards of black firelit sky
Rent by eagle cries and antelope hoots,
There was joy surely, as there is here,

Looking up from an armchair, approaching forty,
At this pair of newly polished wooden heads,
Brought home from East Africa,

With a role of super eight and bagfuls of negatives—
One of them, developed, enlarged,
Mounted, nailed and hung up to reveal

This creased sleeping lion,
Reported to have been heard at dawn,
Snoring outside the tent I was conceived in.

Sequence Addressed to Hanging Objects

I

PUNCHING BAG

Yes, I have come back, though I said I wouldn't,
And not for blows, this time, only words.
Your taut knotted cords have swung back,
As always, to the quiet centre they started from,
Creaking back, in my absence, to those heavy,
Pendulous silences I no longer wish to break.
And the brief creases I made in your tough leather skin
Have evened themselves out with their usual ease,
Leaving me, as always, at odds with myself,
The same unvictorious, unvanquished soliloquiser
Who left here half an hour ago,
With no denouement to enact, no epiphany
In the making, no sublime finality to arrive at
Or return to; though thankfully,
I still have a confession to make.
I had thought, on my way back here, to begin with:
Come, let us be friends, or,
I have come back to make peace with you,
Yet find myself wholly unprepared for this,
My words as useless as my knuckles have been,
Having never really forgiven you
For being so unlike me, for not asking me,
Even once, to unclench my love, unglove my fists,
And smoothen with a caress

The tenebrous hollows I made in your thick yellow hide.
What I have done to you, I confess, I have done out of envy,
Denying life more deeply at every punch,
Denouncing my fate for having clad me in flesh;
For I have wanted little more, all this while,
Than to become like you,
Sealed, as you are,
Beyond taking offence or feeling abused,
Not caring to be loved,
Unloving, inanimate,
Unhurt.

II

DREAM CATCHER

What it is about you
That makes your presence so hard to abide,
I simply don't get:
Either you have no effect whatsoever,
Or you've got things figured out
Differently from me.
That bead at the heart of your circled cross,
Strapped by the hands of a Navajo squaw,
And blessed, perhaps, before it was sold
For ten dollars at a souvenir shop,
Has not caught in its little globe of red
Such thoughts as seem worth sleeping over.
Nor have your feathers,
Plucked from the plumage of a hunted raven,
Winged from my sleep what I long to outgrow.
Your indifference towards the living

Continues to amaze me,
And I am amazed, each morning,
At the alacrity with which you waken the dead,
Returning them, unsummoned by me,
To their old homes in my nerves.
Perhaps you are doing this to test me,
Because I cannot bring myself
To believe in you enough—
But at least for tonight, grant me a future,
A dream of something still to be done,
A word to be spoken, the prospect of a song.
Grant me a nightmare, if you must,
But do something, for God's sake,
Do something.

III

WIND CHIME

So you are at it again: luring me away
From this swirling welter of splintered thoughts,
Towards the thought of thoughtlessness.
Your light, tremulous tones
That add up to no tune
Though they are never off-key,
And your jagged, unmeditated rhythms,
Wrought by no mind of wood, wind and tempered steel,
Have always urged me to listen for silences
I cannot hear;
Though I still cannot tell,
After all our years together,
Which I would prefer:

To be able at last to give myself to the wind,
Or to simply have no self to give.
I think of all those breezeless afternoons,
When you hung in silence at my window—
Not caring to be touched, not asking to be stirred—
While I lay upon the couch, anxiously still,
Searching for ways to impersonate the wind;
Sultry, listless afternoons,
When I grew tired of waiting,
And longed to stir your motionless bars,
Though there was no telling
What my breath would make them do.
And I remember also those gusty nights,
When your thin bars quivered uncomplainingly,
While I tried so hard to emulate their ways,
Making myself an instrument, divesting myself of personality,
Till your quiet, unassuming tones lulled me to sleep,
Then nudged me awake,
With a fierce, febrile music thrumming through my nerves,
Eager to drown your scattered notes,
In a wilful flourish of well-wrought cadences.
Wind or no wind,
How difficult it was to just listen to you;
To be at home amongst your random harmonies
And follow your wide unscheming silences,
Without needing to make sense of them,
Or to sense amongst them,
The broken beginnings of an imminent tune.
I think of all those promises I made to my ears
Which my tongue did not keep,
And even now, as I speak,
My words begin to smart,
Their echoes deepening, as if these walls were closing in,

And no space large enough
For both of us to inhabit.
I am going out now,
To ease myself of the immediacy of this distance,
Though I know your notes will follow me as I walk,
Creeping up, behind me, in your absence,
Or leading me on, furtively,
Towards the edge of some submission
Never quite arrived at.
As always, I will not know what to do
When I begin to hear them;
But if you could hear me I would have you know,
That when they come over me like that,
As if out of nowhere,
Like the thought of green
On a dead summer morning,
Or the dying memory of a half-forgotten cloud,
They are warm, homely
And briefly comforting.

Apostrophe to a Fondue Pot

Visions of lost comfort gather round you at dusk:
The warm, alluring smell
Of Gruyere, Kirsch and central heating.
The branched candelabra and the two-pronged forks
Diligently burnished by seven.
Brother at homework,
Mother in the kitchen dicing baguettes
And scrubbing you clean for our tall white guests,
The young sycamores laced with early snow.
When we came home to this relentless heat,
We brought you back with us;
And when I left home for good
You were amongst the few things
I took along with me,
A souvenir of times when family meant more
Than a habit one only gave into in sleep,
Or in one's weaker moments when awake.
For years you stayed on the bedroom shelf,
Your copper sides unpolished, your spirit-lamp unlit,
Though the tripod you sat upon
Made you strangely venerable,
A symbol of some imminent communion
Hitherto unknown;
Of an impalpable closeness to continue searching for,
Though I could find no earthly use for you,
Until suddenly, one evening,
The poets began to come over for dinner.
I thought of you at once,
Running to the doctor for surgical spirit,

Chopping garlic fine, grating whatever cheese I could
Lay my hands upon and uncorking dark bottles
Of Goan white wine.
What I poured into you, finally,
Was never quite fondue, in the traditional sense,
But what was important,
Was that you looked exotic, as I fancied I did;
Though unlike me, you also looked wholly inviting,
And knew devilishly well how to play the host
Without stealing the show;
Or without, at least,
Letting your guests know that you were taking over.
Yours was the fire that was to bring us together,
Hauling us out of our stiff, solipsistic selves,
Melting the ancient, unyielding ice in our veins,
Till we could share the comforts of a common tongue
As warm and homely as molten cheese.
I remember stirring the cheese feverishly,
Pouring more wine into it, every now and then,
To make sure it wouldn't get hard,
Though it always did in the end,
Thickening into a crust like some incurable grief
We had all tried so hard to overlook.
How bitterly the young beat poet looked at you
Each time that happened,
The handsome worshipper of Kerouac and Crane,
High on hashish and the smell of his own sweat,
His eyes almost as red as your hot copper rim.
I liked the way he pointed his fork
At the tame undergraduate who quoted Larkin.
Such a studied reverence for the immaculate
Seemed to threaten him.
To be a real poet, he asserted, you had not only

To be born with a forked tongue,
But to be completely unashamed
To lay bare your uncertainty
As to which of its pointed prongs was truly yours.
He was a hard man to put up with,
Let alone understand,
But when he left the country for good
None of us felt relieved,
Not even the lovelorn sonneteer
Who seemed as broken by his hopeless lust for him
As he was impervious to his verse.
Easy to swallow but hard to stomach,
He would say, when he tried to describe it,
But I suspect it was just too pungent
For his honey-seeking tongue,
And too strong an attack upon his need for decorum.
Our sonneteer was a man who wanted poems
To contain him like rooms;
Quiet, high-ceilinged rooms
With drawn blinds and wide floors,
Furnished cautiously with the simplest of comforts
And a few stray indulgences,
Their thick walls a firm bulwark against the riot of his life.
He was probably more easily enticed
By your furtive schemes than the rest of us were,
More anxious than any of us to believe in your promise
Of mutual empathy,
And in the power of words to at once unite and liberate.
There were times when he stared at you,
As if *you* were his whole universe in miniature,
An image he longed to hurl himself inside
And be utterly consumed by—
Though it was strange how each time

He dipped his bread inside you,
He just held it there for ages,
Musing morosely before putting it to his lips,
As if eternity had always lain right there before him,
Between the tip of his fork and the tip of his tongue,
Perpetually deferring some imaginary consummation
He had been longing for since birth.
How shall we tell the consumer from the consumed?—
He once asked me, when we had gone out
To a shopping-mall to buy more wine,
Pompously misquoting the poet he most feared.
I had thought myself credulous until I met *him*;
But his constant need to envision transcendence
Was truly frightening,
And I was relieved to hear,
When he finally began to fall apart,
That the quiet, boy-loving greybeard
Who hadn't published in thirty years
And spent half the year with his wife in Spain,
Had taken him under his wing.
I heard recently, that the young, brittle-boned soliloquiser
Had run off to Spain to stay with his ex-lover's wife.
But so much for him.
I prefer to think of his aging friend;
Of the way he pressed his beard against his shoulder
When he looked at you,
His gaze shifting warily between you and his lover,
As if it had fallen too often, upon too many broken things,
Not to know, even for a minute,
That what both of you claimed to offer
Could be neither given nor received—
Though he still hoped to be blessed
With the sort of communion

One can only experience alone.
He had seen too many visions himself, perhaps,
And for too long,
Or simply seen around him,
Too much of the kind of spirited believing,
That can only bring one to a miserable end,
To succumb boyishly to your guileful stratagems;
And yet, he kept glaring at you
As if you still stood for something worth looking for,
Something he could only find, perhaps,
By turning steadily away from you.
I liked him for liking the heavy doses of garlic chutney
I poured into you;
Though he didn't forget to mention
That it was wholly out of character
With true fondue-culture.
Bombay is too hot for cheese fondue,
He once said, with a tremor, in his voice,
But go ahead if you must,
Every young man's got to do his thing,
And if fondue's your thing,
You've got to do it, no matter what happens.
It still makes me shiver to think
Of the great iced pause that followed that utterance.
For I knew then that our gatherings would soon have to stop;
That words, regardless of what they seemed to be doing,
Could only take us further away from one another,
Though they could also take us deeper, perhaps,
If we let them,
Into the emptiness from which they had sprung—
A fact that the superbly gifted middle-aged woman
Who was amongst us at the time,
Seemed to have known from the start,

Wise, as she was, to your soundless subterfuge;
And alert, each time she glanced at you,
To your well-tried plans for ambush.
She was the only one of the lot
Whom I had liked at once,
If only for not wearing her demons upon her sleeve.
She rarely wore sleeves, for that matter,
And I can't tell if she did that to prove a point,
But I certainly hope she didn't.
It would spoil the marvellously
Self-contained picture I still have of her.
She was a woman with an enviable capacity
For showing restraint, when she sounded most likely
To give way; and she seemed to know,
Before she opened her mouth,
That whomever else she might address,
She was speaking primarily to herself,
Though it was puzzling how she too,
Like all the rest of them,
Left each gathering lonelier than she came,
As if she had given in, privately, while she spoke to us,
To the belief that we could hear her as she did.
I think of all those febrile lines of verse
That flew across you like swift darts of dragonfire;
And of the milder, less conspicuous ones,
That vanished above you like thin curves of smoke;
And wonder what—if you could have felt anything—
You would have made of us then.
You would have felt sorry for us, I suppose,
As I had certainly begun to,
Long before we stopped meeting altogether;
Though possibly—which is more likely—
You would simply have laughed at our stupidity,

Gloating over the masterful stealth
Of each unforeseeable ambuscade;
And the unpracticed ease
With which you had seduced us
Into trusting you.
A month after I last filled you with cheese
I considered giving you away
To someone who might put you
To some less enigmatic use.
And only last Thursday,
I thought of locking you up
In the chest on the loft,
With the family photographs
And my thick black file of unposted letters.
But I have decided instead,
To keep you where you are,
Seated on your tripod upon the living-room shelf:
No longer a symbol of that growing roundedness
And shared surrender I thought worth waiting for,
But simply a reminder of how foolish I have been,
How eager to believe that words,
When they brought us briefly out of ourselves,
Could bring us closer to those outside us,
Waylaid, as I have been, by my own need to be heard,
And by a child's first smell of Kirsch and Gruyere,
Baguettes, Emmental and mild white wine,
With bright silver cutlery, laid immaculately in squares,
And tall white guests over for dinner
At half past seven.

The Schoolboy on the Pont Alexandre III

Looking out across the darkening water,
but finding no sign of the 'great, graceful arch'
his Michelin Guide has promised him he will see,
he begins once again to feel like a bridge.

Here, at last, is what he was born to do:
to span the sad rift
between the gifted and the tone-deaf,
the sober and the merry,
the keepers of accounts
and the votaries of love;

and to sprawl unquestioningly
across strong currents of turbulence,
so his mother can cross home
into the south she dreams of,
his father move out into the sheltering north,
listening unmoved
while he bears their weight,
and they exchange strange words upon their way.

Before him, below him, the river flows on unconcerned.
A mild yellow haze comes over Les Invalides,
and on the way home the quays and markets,
the streets and public squares
seem suddenly full of ways to be.
Night comes companionably upon the Opera Comique,
and it doesn't occur to him until the next morning,
that the bridge he looked out from
was the one he was looking for.

Ostrich Egg

A fortnight after the papers had been signed,
And the old villa stripped of its carpets and furnishings,
Its Mughal miniatures and stone antiques, brass plates,

Photographs and leopard skins, and all its stacks
Of files and letters, he went back there to make sure
Nothing worth keeping had been left behind.

Cacti by the doorstep. The musunda in full bloom.
A flight of stairs whose banisters he slid down
As a child, and a bridge table with a set

Of cold maternal spoons, briefly touched and put down,
In a breeze warm with the scent of unpicked mangoes
Ripe before rain to the point of rotting.

That old crooked ladle? The beef platter?
His grandmother's tattered venetian tablecloth? Perhaps,
But enough had already been taken and kept,

That kept roots frozen in the permafrost of his past.
What had been lived here, in any case, was barely life,
And the man he was moving on to meet,

Would have no need for these.
Where I go now, he mused, *joy will be real*—
Though the betel trees shook their heads in disapproval,

Mocking his customary dreams of emergence,
As he turned his back with rehearsed aplomb,
On an overused kettle, and an unopened set of rusty golf clubs;

And the bougainvilleas caught in the spikes on the garden wall,
Brandished their thorny inflorescences like platitudes,
Forewarning him against all forcing of the will,

When at last he heard the red gates clank shut behind him,
With nothing in his hands,
But a large white egg in a black stone bowl,

That had sat for five decades on his grandfather's desk,
And now finds itself at home, sooner than he does,
In a plush new apartment on the twenty-first floor,

Niched below the Shakespeares on the library shelf,
And between the brass figurines and a salvaged demijohn:
Speckled, light-reflecting oracle,

Dome-shaped demigod
Sporting its curious message of continuance and hope
For a life of taciturn sunsets and talkative nights,

Visionary noons and companionable dawns,
All doomed to remain no more real,
Than the long curved neck and scrawny legs,

The beak and claws,
The stride, squawk, charge and leap,
And the ineffable flightless plumage

Of an ostrich that must stay unalterably unborn.

Hangman's Knot

So we meet again,
And not in sleep, this time, but awake after midnight,
Your eyes fixed hard upon the featureless space
My curves enclose,
More envious now, of my facelessness,
Than they were in your dreams;
You who are your own hangman,
Your hands deceived, each by the other's guile,
Betrayed by an emptiness that neither could hold,
Taut, deluded, unloving hands,
That took me out of the kitchen cupboard,
Less than half an hour ago,
Fondling my frayed unknotted strands,
Then closing around me into a fist,
As if they had found at last,
In what they suddenly clasped,
Their one true love.

***

Yes, make me a symbol if you must,
Your God, your messiah,
Or the flawless zero of your being.
Summon me with reverence, implore me for release,
Or call me a mere object, if you prefer,
A mindless tool, the unwitting
Instrument of a self-wrought deliverance,
A tragic knot, a magic knot,
A veritable miracle of a knot,
Or the one certain, undeniable knot

That can untie the thousand you cannot see:
The great knot of memory interwoven with desire,
Of desire wound around itself
And of love writhing to let itself loose
From coils of its own, artless, making—
Yet make of me what you will,
I remain,
Despite your efforts to prove me otherwise,
No more or less than I have always been,
Neither space nor circumference, god nor cipher,
And no part of the emptiness my curves contain,
Merely an uncertain length of rope,
Partially in love with itself.

***

Look, human, upon the bright tiled floor,
Where the wooden stool you were about to climb,
Clutch and kick to your own undoing,
Stands silent in a garden of mosaic flowers.
Can you not see that they have begun to move,
That they have been moving all this while, in spite of you,
In spite of your stubborn, unsurrendering lust
For an imagined stillness you will never know?
No certain music fills this living air;
And yet, all space grows habitable
As you lose yourself in it,
Till old misgivings become forgotten acquaintances,
And wide floors irresolutely paced across,
Bright mirrors looked into as often
As they were turned away from,
Low ceilings, shelves and rafters hopelessly gazed at,
Doors slammed tight and anxiously forced open,
Cushions, blinds, tables and windows

Become new-found friends.
These walls and all that lies outside them,
Are more at home in your veins
Than you have dared envision;
And all things have their voices.
Listen, and you may find
We have more in common than meets the eye,
That you and I are two of a kind:
You, who have believed me to be,
Not face, but mere contour;
And me,
Whom you have believed to be
All matter and no mind.
Unbind yourself, human,
Unwind, unwind.

The Sun Made Flesh

I

KUNTI REMINISCES

Orange had always been my favourite colour.
The earthy, unimportunate orange
Which the sun cast, absent-mindedly,
Before revealing himself,
The mustard-fields aglow with his unassuming light.
It was partly because of this that I summoned him,
Partly because I wondered, as all children do,
If it were light or the eye that made things visible.
I thought the sun could tell me for certain,
And believed he would come to me as I had imagined him,
A being composed entirely of light,
Though gifted with speech.
The sage had warned me, when he taught me the strange words,
To be in no great hurry to use them,
To choose a propitious time with care;
Yet how could I have known, tutored as I was,
In neither love nor prophecy,
That words alone,
Which had seemed so trifling till then,
Could wield such power,
That mere words,
Given to a child by an aging sage,
As if they were only new toys to play with,
Could bring about such things,

Compelling a god to fulfil his lust
Against his own will:
The sun made flesh,
Piercing my mortal loins with more than mere light.
Was this the seer's idea of a joke?
Or had he forgotten how curious a young girl
Could be, about things he no longer cared for?
Ever since that morning I have been a lover of the dark,
An incurable seeker
Of tenebrous spaces in which to brood;
Cold, penitential spaces, where I could dare envision
The son I abandoned amongst the riverside reeds,
Whom I never dared, while he lived, to call my own.
My son, whom I left there, with no-one to protect him,
Yet swaddled in an armour that was quite his own,
His earrings glistening in the sun they came from.
How often, since that morning, I have thought of the sun
As someone worshipful though terrible to behold;
Someone I could trust to look over our son,
Guiding him by subtle signs,
Without fully revealing himself;
And yet, in all these years, I have never dared
To think of him simply as someone I had loved,
Boldest, as I have been, before midnight,
Most cautious at noon,
When my shadow curled into me,
And I trembled to think,
Pressing my secret even closer to my heart,
That the light I shone by was not mine.
History will have its way, making of this what it will,
Saying what it must,
Remembering in the most memorable of rhymes,
What I have longed to forget,

Speaking of me, perhaps,
As a selfish woman, inexorably weak,
Though born of a heroic line.
It is some comfort to think that my son,
Whose ends I always thwarted in life,
Has earned in death the fame he sought;
Yet so much for posterity.
It has never mattered to me as much as it did to him.
My concern remains, as before, with the living,
For I am still amongst them;
Though I have little left to do now,
Having lived too long in fear of light,
But play out my one heroic deed,
Which is one that no-one will ever get to hear of:
Today, I will not shirk the sun's brisk advances,
But endure his terrible coming with pride,
Summoning him home, once again, into my eyes,
As I did our firstborn, a few weeks before he died.
Now time, having done its worst,
Has little left to destroy.
Night gives way unreluctantly to orange,
And dawn comes gently over the mustard fields.

II

KARNA, ON GIVING UP HIS ARMOUR

In the end, it wasn't half as difficult
As I thought it would be.
The sun, whom I have always revered
Above all the other gods,
Had warned me in my sleep of the great king's coming,

And I had known beforehand what he would ask for,
Which is probably what made it difficult in the first place.
I have always been a giver of gifts,
And a proud one at that.
Yet before today, whenever I have given myself,
It has just happened on impulse,
The unsought moment getting the better of me,
When I least expected it to—
As when the insect bit my thigh,
And I bore the pain quietly,
Simply to let my mentor sleep;
Or at the tournament, when I gave my heart to the prince,
Without his having to ask for it.
Each time,
The impulse to give took me by surprise,
And I thought of nothing, at the time,
But the joy it gave me,
Caring little for what might come of it later.
This time, however, things were different.
The sun's midnight visitation left me disturbed,
Forewarned, in part, of today's events,
And pacing about, irresolutely, till noon,
When my choice could no longer be delayed.
I made up my mind the minute I saw him:
The king of rain and heaven in mendicant robes—
Though I did not know he would offer me
Anything in return.
When he granted me a wish, I asked him for his strength,
For I need to be strong to be true to my love,
Though knowledge of my origins is what I long for most,
Haunted, as I am,
By the unsolved mystery that still pulses through my veins.
Was I wrong to put my name before my love?

I chose my fame as a giver instead of true martyrdom,
Which would have required me simply
To hold on to what I had;
And yet, having done this, I feel no guilt but joy,
Looking back contentedly upon that minute,
When the heavens showered petals upon my choice.
For I am glad to be relieved of those gifts I was born with,
Which have clung to me, since birth, to keep me from death,
Dipped, as they were, in the bitter drink of immortality.
My hands rejoice to know, for the first time,
What my bare chest feels like,
Naked, at last, in this ebbing light; and the sun,
Before he sinks below the edge of the west,
Gazes proudly on my refusal to survive.

Lament of an Onanist Bemused by the Void

Why do you send me all this neo-dervish drivel instead of poems?
—Vivek Narayanan

I start things well but end them wrong.
Is that death I sense at the edge of this bed?
I end with a shout I cannot prolong.

Who lies here in pain and this purple sarong,
Myself or the meat on which old hungers fed?
I start things well but end them wrong.

That fabled quiescence at the core of song,
Is it here, in the flesh, or reserved for the dead?
I end with a shout I cannot prolong.

To whom does the zero at the peak belong?
Shall I follow, with these feet, its motionless tread?
I start things well but end them wrong,

Marooned by the surge that drowns this throng
Of raucous images at war in my head.
I end with a shout I cannot prolong.

The void can sing, for sure, but not for long—
O do not ask where that music fled—
I start things well but end them wrong;
I end with a shout I cannot prolong.

Ablutions

Each morning, lying back in bed, I sing my first note.
My demon sings his, standing at my door.

He never stops when I start,
Though I close my lips soon enough

To take in his finer trills and smoother glissandos,
His steadier rhythms and bolder flourishes.

He is a better singer than I am,
I concede.

His vowels are rounder,
His humming more audible,

His frills are more decorous,
His tremolo more subtle.

He has a broader tone, a huskier bass,
A more stentorian upper octave,

An instant mellifluous retort
To the most arcane musical question

I can think of posing, a louder bellow,
A sharper twang, purer pitch and yet,

He remains completely dumbfounded
Each time I ask him

Why he never dares follow me into the shower.
Does he flinch from water because he fears—

For all his bravado and brash virtuosity—
That being drenched in something more tactile

Than he can ever hope to be,
Might be too much for him,

That he would perish at its touch?
Or can he simply not bear to see

How comfortable I now am
With my own nakedness,

How willing I turn
To be seized by water

And give myself to the stark and craftless rapture
Of this chill awakening?

I muse, pacifically, upon the sober comforts
Of being human, perishable, and clad in my own flesh;

And ask of all that host of demons
That have made their homes

In the frenzied nerves of this world's singers,
Since the first song sprang forward,

And the first note broke from the human throat,
Who, amongst them, can rob me now

Of this growing presence,
This minute's reprieve?

From *Waking in December*
(2001)

Ithaca

So we were to go there together—
Our heads dizzy with ouzo,
Lulled asleep by the Adriatic between Brindisi and Patras.
Together, we were to return to that clear blue motherland
Neither of us had known—
A homeland neither Penelope's nor Odysseus', nor even Cavafy's,
But serenely our own.
Sparta would drench us in Mediterranean heat,
The Peloponnesus sparse yet content to be lived in—
For we were to go there not at once
But the long way round, surprised at each halt
Yet certain we were getting there;
To lose one another at Epidavros
And meet suddenly on stage, though unmasked and playing no part,
Our palms not sentient of what they longed to clutch,
But wound around each other like the wand of Aesculapius,
A single healing hand.
History would not tempt us upon the hill of Corinth,
As we scaled the bare crags of Aphrodite,
To share amidst her ruins a hermit's solitary love—
And Athens would find us studiously unclassical,
The caryatids weary of wondering
If they were women or mere columns,
Cured of their longing to be more than pure stone.
No oracles would daunt us, no memories lure us,
When we took ship from Piraeus,
Drawn by no sirens but our own low humming,
As the Cyclades wove themselves into a choral chant,
Oblivious of the straits that lay between them;

And no dreams would follow us into Mycenae,
Urging her lions to outleap their stone and roar,
No words echo the stillness of Agamemnon's tomb
As we fell asleep, at once together and alive.
Yet such is the way of journeys—
The best ones are those never begun.
Ithaca, dream-home of the idle, dark hope of the damned, goodbye...
I will live here alone by this muddy brown sea
Till I outlive the lure of your unseen shores;
For here, between these sand-ribs and high fronds of palm,
There is more to listen for than what cannot be heard;
Here gullcry and wingbeat syncopate at dusk,
And surf murmurs in my ears its wordlesss drone.

To the Face of an Infant Seen through a Fish Tank

Pisces Restaurant, Nana Chowk

You like them—
The little white ones with the pink-tipped fantails?
Well, if you could hear me I would tell you—
I like them too—and here comes another—
A long blue one this time,
Catching the light with a swish of its fins
Before it catches your eye,
The seaweed glittering as if nature had always meant it to.
Yes, there are some strange things here, aren't there,
In this glass cage we find each other on opposite sides of:
You, tugging at your father's sleeve,
Your lower lip rising to your tiny milk teeth to say—*fish*—
As if these dumb creatures had only been
Swimming about here for you to say that word.
I would cross over to your side and tell you
About a little brave boy who turned into a fish,
And swam out into the sea till he no longer felt afraid—
But you are least interested in what my lips might be babbling
To either of us, smeared like my fingers, with the thick brown gravy
Of a curried black pomfret—
My hands empowered with a strength yours lack,
Yet powerless to sense the newness of this pane as yours do.
For all you could care I might be as dumb as a fish—
Which makes me feel a bit left out, of course,
Though your indifference, I must confess, is wise;
For I can tell you little honestly about fish
But that some of the small ones grow into big ones

And that the big ones eat the ones that don't,
And that try as one may,
No-one can see either as anyone else does.
Yet sleep, little cherub, unhatched incubus,
Unhampered by such unhappy musings,
As the rickshaw your father now lifts you into
Rocks you home;
And be in your dreams a part of this vast watery world,
Not one who stands outside it, unable to get in—
But one whose fins the seaweed tickles,
As light air-bubbles, and the brown tails of guppies,
And the bright scales of goldfish pass him by.

Creepers on a Steel Door

Three months now, creeping up this door,
Half-open, between myself and the garden-yard.
I wonder, why at times, it is so hard,
To reach the wide world across the narrow floor.

Space must have its bounds, I suppose,
Though the heart's first impulse be to leap.
The creeper does not wish to move, it simply grows—
It is the eye that makes these broad leaves creep.

But see how tight each tendril grips the grill,
Where the highest leaves, translucence-shy, peep inside.
I can tell what makes them want to hide;
Could they hear, I would tell them—looking in can kill.

Departure

I see them across the rim of a fogged lens,
Amidst the swivelling glare of party lights—
Too bright now, now too dark, to do
What they have asked me to: these two,
Arm in arm, their eyes aslant with impatient poise,
Awaiting the brief redemption of a flash—
Now? Perhaps, but I am a poor photographer,

And prefer to see what open eye and shutter
Conspire so closely to conceal:
Her, fastening her seat-belt three nights hence,
Content to believe, as she leans to the left
To watch grey buildings grow tiny below her,
That her flight home is also a journey out.
She is not thinking of the man who wades

Through the familiar spaces of her absence,
Into the exquisite hovel of his home,
Floundering, lip-deep, in the gravy of speech,
As he reaches out for the lost island of the flesh:
Words that may conjure the ghost of a caged green bird,
Who never answered back, even when alive—Quick—
My fingers say, as they tighten, and click.

Toy Store Window

Closer and more real than news of a war
Fought on frontiers I will never see,
Through smooth wet panes toy soldiers confront me,
Caught in the rain outside this store. Once more
Now, my fingers slide across the icy glass,
As if behind it lay a world once mine,
Though we together were bound to pass—
A world of plastic soldiers in a line,
Guarding a great grey castle on a hill.
Dying was a game we played together,
Then rose in an instant at my will,
To meet the enemy in darker weather.
I stationed my men at their posts,
And took for myself the high watchtower.
Grey armies drew towards us like timeless ghosts,
And a low gong rang to announce the hour,
As campfires rose in the dying light.
I thought my arrows would never miss;
As I stood watching from that height,
I saw strange things far-off but never this:
Myself looking back through a window pane
At toys like those I thought my own;
My shadow groping to grasp in vain,
The unlooked-for man into whom I have grown.

Nocturne

Dusk and the ghats were behind us when we reached the river—
Summer had drained it of all motion, but its grey
Surfaces were still cold and clear. I watched you shiver
As we undressed. We swam, and between the algae
The moon swam with us like a silver
Fish—then sank into the silt like a broken plate,
As your fingers ruffled the summer-still river.
Reflection made it more distant, and we had no bait
With which to catch the quick inflections of its light—
Only the taut insistence of memory.
How long it seemed till the water resettled, and sight
Pieced together again that cracked porcelain moon. We
Swam, bare as ourselves and the river we swam in—
Then deep in the shallows dead still we lay.
You will remember this now though you were looking away:
Us wading ashore through the river's wet skin,
And clouds roll below us like shoals of grey salmon.

In Praise of Bone

Somewhere at the back of the brain,
Is a place I will never go to again;
An old stone guardhouse long deserted,
And over the slow green spaces of a lily-pond skirted
By rock, quick breeze and a low murmur of reeds.
The rocks are large and flat. I look up from the weeds
Wedged between their edges; his eyes are too full of love.
Was that a monsoon gathering above,
Or the liquescent dead come to be with us again?
High noon is about us when it begins to rain,
And we grow as tangled as a banyan tree;
Marrow will outlive its bone—
We are plant, animal, stone,
And everything we believe ourselves to be.
When the rain stops he only feels my skin
To know my bones are still the same shape;
The same hard forms we will never escape,
We know in the end only they can win:
Somewhere at the back of my brain—
A place I may not visit, the onset of rain.

To an Aging Sarod Player

Technique hardly mattered once you got started—your only guide
Was what you had to say—your fingers grown so old,
Each note slipped by before you could unfold it;
And yet, I thought it bold—the way you tried

To sound—proud as ever, still unsatisfied
By those purer tones you will never reach again.
Only once shame caught hold of you—and even then,
I loved the way your fingers cried:

You, turning your face away from me, longing to hide,
Till between two strokes your eyes meet mine. *Friend*,
They say, *neither love nor music will ever end,*
So long as time is busy changing things outside.

Dawn—and I wonder if your fingers lied;
An early bus-ride through dimly moving streets,
Then bright sun gilding the morning tide. All night,
Time had been busy changing things outside.

Chandri Villa

His name was Chandri—my grandfather once said—
Who was to live here, but died of plague. Each of us fails
In the end, but I was born in a house built for the dead:
On the red gate they hammered his name with nails.

Nineteen Nineteen. These bougainvilleas
Have grown since then; the dead leave us, leaving no trails—
Deep in the banyan-grove at Chandri Villa,
A secret sense of loss prevails.

And the very stillness of these trees carries me past an April
Long dead, newly strewn with banyan leaves; thick roots dangle
Above my head—ancient, knotted roots I cannot untangle,
Till I am a child once again though against my will,

The wide grove closing its arms as if to kill;
My veins so many banyan roots twisted into one,
And all their tangled knots come undone,
Till almost I see him—the plagued man I never will.

Harbour Crossing

Beyond the bay—about half a mile of surf and wind—
The last bus awaits us at Ferry Wharf.
The island is a cyclops about to sleep; behind,
The hunched mainland shrinks into a dwarf.

So, to put it bluntly, we are neither here nor there.
The moon seems to understand this, pretending once again
To be young, rolling herself into an orange flare
As you speak of Greece and a bluer sea; then

Dark flags, prows, and green meshes drift between,
And over the sea her charred beams are sparse;
You do not ask what this worn-out scenery might yet mean—
Let this remain—you say, and watch them pass,

Till slowly over the docks the moon returns to grey,
Salvages from time a minute—then anchors us to Bombay.

In Praise of Laterality

Happy the polished surface of a wooden desk,
And the stacked flat strips of a drawn cane blind,

Whose thin threads bind and divide them like longitudes,
Only to allow them to stay this way—

This is the hour of resignation,
When walls no longer exist to shut space in,

But simply for white beams to rest upon,
While shelves grow meaningful in themselves,

Or purely for being parallel to ceiling and floor—
As if standing idols and glass decanters,

Collected works and copper jars,
Were merely weights to test their strength against—

The strength of flatness against the will to rise;
Now lulled by the comfort of wall-to-wall matting

As I contemplate the smoothness of cold stone tiles,
How disturbing it is to remind myself,

That the earth is round, and spins

Monologue of a Piece of Coal

Here, at the heart of time's highest mountain,
Buried alive, at birth, amidst roots of stone,
Pale stalactites grow coldly towards me
Like portents of an imminent weight
I thought myself born to bear;
The sudden crashing thud of it—then the slow
Pounding of all I am into little bright bits of me—
But I have dreamt too often now,
Of the passing lure of the miner's hand,
The craftsman's keen eye looking right through me
As his scalpel rids me of what he thinks
I do not need.
There is a certain thrill in it, of course—
The sheer giddiness of being filled with light,
And the pride one might take
In hardening oneself slowly—
Yet leave me where I am, Earth;
And leave outside where it may be;
For I wish no more to see myself
Than I desire to scatter light—
Only to be at ease in my own opacity;
I, who am the darkest of the dark,
And want to keep what is mine.

Kaleidoscope

Behold—I have done it again;
Neither miracle nor accident,
Merely an old trick played in an entirely new way.
You who believe you have been watching me change,
Unwatched by me,
As I turn in strange palms around nothingness—
Vain eye, deluded seer,
Seeking trite symmetries in a flux of light,
Rummaging through this boundless rage of shape,
For the faintest semblance of an order,
Will you ever finally come to terms with me?

Catch me if you can—but I am too quick for you—
Wide hairy lid, tardy onlooker,
You I hold still, suspended in the space
Between a glance and a blink,
Hurling colour like dust at your neat white curves,
As I assume, at your will, a form you cannot guess.

No, don't get me wrong, not even for a second,
I am neither God nor an image of him;
A mere contraption put together to fulfil
The pitiful pettiness of a human necessity—
Wishful eye, rash believer,
You in whom love seeks a form,
I will never quite become what you want me to be,
Nor will you suffer to leave me as I am.

But put me down if you can—
Come on, I defy you to do it, once and for all—
Let go of infinity with a final shake,
And never ask yourself again
What may have become of me;
How round or pointed or straight I may have turned,
Or how purple or green or blue or brown—
Just put me down.

Villanelle

Unveil the mirror and begin to see
What visions deny before the eye laid bare—
Or if the mirror be a veil, let it be.

Were these the eyes that woke at noon to see
White wings leap free from a winding stair?
Unveil the mirror and begin to see.

Now dark comes down on what I have longed to be—
A thing at home in its own despair;
If the mirror be a veil, let it be.

But climb if you dare; flight takes the free,
The spirit too light for the flesh to bear;
Unveil the mirror and begin to see

If love arise where all images flee
A self dismantled beyond repair—
Or if the mirror be a veil, let it be.

Now pluck from the heart the poison-tree,
And watch unmoved what is moving there;
Unveil the mirror and begin to see—
Or if the mirror be a veil, let it be.

The Thing Itself

for Ranjit Hoskote

No hope of redemption beyond bone and flesh,
Or benediction from the blue vaults
Of the compassionate dead; nothing
That does not lie here, naked, before the eye,
Nor even the thought of it—they said,
The yellow monks in red: just
Sunlight on a tree obscured by dust.

What meets the pure eye is as nameless as you are,
As little concerned with the vastness of things,
A wordless thing that has nothing to say—
At once—they said—take it in as it is,
While being is fluid, lest the self take shape,
And stiffen, like wet clay, into a crust—
Sunlight on a tree obscured by dust.

Sight ends with seeing—only vision survives, to screen
The hurt eye from the hard stare of the visible—
Yet is that peace—to live and look and long for
No meaning in what the eye sees—the random
Delight of a selfless eye? I live amongst words,
For they are friendlier, and easier to trust,
Than the light on a tree obscured by dust.

Light sways with the tree—a shimmering chiaroscuro;
I feel the haze quiver, yet take this as a sign,
And rejoice to be where I have chosen to be;
For here, in the half-dark of words, like any man in love,
I desire to believe what I love my own—
And care no more to be cured of that lust,
Than the light on a tree obscured by dust.

Words to an Aspiring Surrealist

So you persist, I see, in being wilfully rash—
In paying with pages of unbridled balderdash
For a drag of hashish and the afterscent of ash

Shared by no stranger at the end of a line.
Personally, though I admit, your verse sounds fine,
I'd settle for a glass of home-made wine—

Just enough to make surfaces more bearable,
A lost face more tender, a wooden table
Less rough, and dying slowly more endurable;

You have good reason, perhaps, to somnambulate
In sonorous oblivion past the self you hate—
Yet what the dark brings to light may not wait

Till you outlive your delight in danger.
What is likely to last does more than linger,
And the bones of verse, my friend, are stronger

Than the half-burnt nerves of speech peeled bare,
Or that vague final image which is never quite there;
Your verse, like you, needs looking after—take care.

What I Can Get Away With

Let me get this down before I forget—
Time may not recover a forgotten rhyme;
But what I can get away with you can never get.

There will be time to think things over, time for regret,
Time for other lovers and hangovers at dawn;
But let me get this down before I forget.

I should have told you this when we first met:
I'm a performing seal without a soul—
So let me get this down before I forget.

The bet unmade, the truth unsaid, the unpaid debt,
And the same black lies blanched by new moons—
What I can get away with you can never get.

But let's not get upset, my pigeon, my little pet,
Not being a poet, or in love, isn't all that bad;
Though I can get away with what you can never get,

My muse may not wait for the perfect pirouette
Of a half-meant phrase flawlessly turned;
So let me get this down before I forget,

Before you spread your charms about me like a net;
Though your arms have a way of making me feel small,
And your eyes are adept at making me forget

The rent I could not pay, the heart I would not let,
The lines I do not mean but think it fine to say—
What I can get away with you can never get.

But damn, it's gone again. My brains are too wet—
This whiskey's pretty good, though the waiters aren't too bright,
And what they will get away with I will never get.

Another cigarette? No, my little friend, no need to fret,
I'll be with you in a minute, but not just yet;
Just let me get this down before I forget—
What I can get away with you will never get.

Study

The heart's a glass jar with an air-lock;
Wine ferments slowly.

At first the bubbles rise,
Frothing furiously to get out—
Then slowly,
Till you cannot see,
Only hear them—
If you press an ear close to the rim;

And then you can't even hear them—
And you can drink the wine.

Aubade

Now worn, drenched, wrung and hung up to dry,
Heavy, yet flat and bodiless as peace—
My neighbour's white shirts upon this line.

Water Cabbages

Still as painted coracles tied to no shore,
It is not by holding their breaths they do it,
Little green cups brimful of the moon—

Nor is it any concern of theirs,
Content from the start with surfaces,
Desiring to believe no motion their own,
If deep in the mud, where the moon does not reach,
A newly-hatched tadpole is trying to swim;

Rooted in no soil,
And with nothing to do but float and wait,
Till at the lash of a guppy's tail,
A single ripple sets them adrift.

Lines to an Ex-Lover's Pet Tortoise

This glass I lift to you, my friend,
Though you have been less of a friend to me than a mentor,
And would not care to hear me if you could—
Nor would it concern you in the least,
Being at home wherever you are,
That where you now are was once home for me,
Or as close to home as I have come.
Your indifference to the act of love was admirable,
And our petty human antics didn't impress you one bit:
Us taking turns turning turtle on the couch;
Briefly becoming one another's shells,
Yet neither quite losing nor finding ourselves,
As we crawled gaspingly in and out of each other's grasp,
Half-hoping you would pop out your head and watch;
For what we shared, was at its most intense,
Still something of a performance—
A love cold yet comfortable,
Timed as immaculately as a neoclassical duet,
And all the more homely for its dispassion.
I remember those sultry cloudless monsoon nights,
When the rain, by not falling,
Saved me from a sense of my own vacancy,
The need to fill it with a little wisp of longing
For things to be otherwise than they were;
Clear, loveless nights on which—
My lover fast asleep and hardly still there
I had only you and the moon for company,
And could not tell which of you was the more distant;
Her, brandishing herself across taut leagues of darkness,

Anxious to be seen,
Or you, tucked up as usual inside yourself,
Three feet from where I lay—
And I remember also the wild, black, stormy nights,
When the rain, hammering impetuously upon the fibreglass roof
Would not leave me even briefly alone—
Me, longing at once to fall asleep and shake my lover awake,
But doing neither.
How hopelessly I tried then to study
The ponderousness of your slow moves across the balcony,
Wondering, when you flexed a muscle,
How much thought must have gone into it,
Envying the swiftness of your retreat into yourself,
And your unlaboured skill at staying put—
For watching you, rock-still, by the moss-covered parapet,
I could suppose contentment was more than a well-played pose;
That below the firm curves of your hard home,
There lay a repose that made longevity desirable—
Yet how impossible it was to tell when you were just about to move;
For you always did it when my thoughts had gone astray—
Though I think I almost caught you at it once,
Peering warily through a pair of wet lettuce leaves
As you put out a limb, then gazing lazily
Across a floor of glazed tiles, as if there were miles between you
And the bedroom door, and no real need to go.
I might have seen things then as I thought you did—
But long nights of lying awake and an unwelcome morning light
Had brought me to believe it was time to be leaving.
I have been studying hard since then,
The quiet wisdom of your ways;
Taking tutelage from you, long-distance,
In the wordless craft of self-containment; learning better,
Perhaps, in your absence, what closeness could not teach—

Though I have also been secreting slowly,
A secret carapace of sentences in which to live;
And have taken lately to flinging words at things,
Spider-like, hoping they will cling somewhere,
Bringing us, however briefly, together.
This one's still for you, chum—though I wonder, at times,
As I crawl from one shell into another,
Never quite at home in my homelessness,
My tongue licking itself dry
Of the sticky home-spun gossamer of speech
As it veers towards the taste of home-made wine,
If all this while, you have been not wise, but simply frightened.

A Leave-Taking

They have begun to say I must be going now,
The half-heard voices at the back of the head;
To do it at once and for my own good:
You I sought out to be alone in,
Whose loneliness could not bear to leave me alone;
Space once longed for,
Neither wholly lived in nor quite outlived,
Are you the same I chanced upon a season ago,
Your grey walls unpainted as if newly-built?
I had thought, if it should come to this,
To strip you bare of those things I gave you
To hide your bareness from my eyes;
Bright prints of impressionist masterpieces,
Hung above photographs of myself,
Flat shelves bent by the weight of words
Neither of us needed to read;
And your broad orange bedspread, as yet
Unruffled by the touch of unfamiliar fingers;
Of these I had thought to relieve you,
Yet choose now neither to clean nor clear you up before I go,
And to take nothing with me but your leave,
To leave you as locked up inside yourself
And full of your own emptiness as I have been,
Your corners echoless, your floor unpaced,
Your carved mirrors with no face to reveal, no self to hide,
Your high windows with no-one to look out through,
Past creeper, fern and barbed wire fence,
Into a neighbourless yard—
Till strange hands unlock a familiar latch

And your clocks chime in someone else's ears,
Still out of time with one another,
As your rafters look down upon, and your blinds close in
On someone else's love. Goodbye, room, goodbye,
It has taken me years to become a part of you—
And will take more than time to take us apart;
The wilful surrender of a hard-clutched self—
Or a single brisk step, correctly taken
Across this floor, past the last mile-containing tile
Between myself and my sandals at your door;
More skill surely than it takes
To make new words about old mistakes,
And more of being left undisturbed, for me to meet myself,
Than cobwebs take to cover the distance
Between ceiling and shelf.

Acknowledgements

Some of these poems were first published in various journals and anthologies:

'Chandri Villa' in *Literature Alive* (British Council, 1994); 'Tidal Wave' in *Journal of Postcolonial Writing* (August 2007, UK) and in *New Quest* (Issue 168, Pune, 2007); 'Elephant Bathing' in *Poetry Wales* (Summer Issue, 2002, Bridgend, Wales, UK); 'Kunti Reminisces' in *New Quest* (Issue 167, Pune, 2007); 'Glacier', 'Dead At Your Mother's Funeral' and 'Vacillations Of A Recondite Nudist' in *Fulcrum 3* (Cambridge, MA, USA, 2004); 'Ablutions' in *Fulcrum 4, Give The Sea Change And It Shall Change: Fifty-six Indian Poets* (Cambridge, MA, USA, 2005); ' Bitter Gourd', 'Living Room', and 'Negotiating Negativity on the Western Ghats', in *Both Sides Of The Sky* (National Book Trust, India, 2008); 'Dancing Girl' in *Poetry With Prakriti* (Prakriti Foundation, Chennai, 2009); 'Puppet's Life Ends on String' in *New Soundings in Postcolonial Writing* (Brill Rodopi, 2016); 'Threesome', 'Two Miniatures' and 'Waterhole' in *The Penguin Book of Indian Poets* (Penguin, 2022). All other poems from the sections entitled 'From Seven Deaths and Four Scrolls', 'From Elephant Bathing', 'Mughal Sequence', and 'From Waking in December' first appeared in print in *Seven Deaths and Four Scrolls* (Poetrywala, 2017), *Elephant Bathing* (Poetrywala, 2012), *Mughal Sequence* (Poetrywala 2012) and *Waking in December* (Harbour Line, 2001) respectively.

The titles 'Puppet's Life Ends on String' and 'Buddhist Monk Hangs Self' are newspaper captions borrowed from *The Times of India* and *The New Indian Express* respectively.

I would like to thank Jerry Pinto, Ranjit Hoskote, Arundhathi Subramaniam and Ritu Khiwani for all their assistance in the emergence of this book; Ravi Shankar for his generous introduction; and Menka Shivdasani for her valuable editorial insights and comments on the text. Special thanks to Vineetha Mokkil for her patience and perseverance as an editor.

www.ingramcontent.com/pod-product-compliance
Lightning Source LLC
LaVergne TN
LVHW041932070526
838199LV00051BA/2783